Rosemary Verey's Making of a Garden

Rosemary Verey's Making of a Garden

Photographs by Tony Lord

Plans rendered in watercolour by Hilary Wills

FRANCES LINCOLN PUBLISHERS

*I dedicate this book to my father-
and mother-in-law, the late
Reverend Cecil Verey and his wife
Linda, and to my husband, the late
David Verey who inspired me to
create this garden, and to our family,
Charles and Denzil, Chris and
Jenny, Veronica, Davina and Hal,
and to their children, Imogen, Nat,
Tasha and Josh, Robert and
Anthony, Lily, Rowan and Amy,
who have worked and played in
the garden.*

HALF TITLE PAGE *The gothick
summer house seen through
the archway in spring time.*

FRONTISPIECE AND LEFT *Yellow
laburnum and mauve alliums in
the laburnum walk are a perfect
colour combination.*

Contents

In the Beginning

I first visited Barnsley House one August weekend in 1939. I wish I could remember the garden more clearly as it was when I saw it then, but at twenty I was more interested in tennis than in gardening. I have a clear picture of the crazy paving path running from the house to a solid wooden gate in a Cotswold stone wall – the way to the tennis court. There were herbaceous borders, young yew hedges and rose beds underplanted with pansies. The field beyond was old ridge-and-furrow, grazed by cows and horses.

In 1940, married to David and expecting our first baby, I lived here from May until September. I remember days in the garden and a summer of sunshine, a backdrop to the threat of air-raids and invasion – and talk of 'digging for victory' should we need to depend for survival on our home-grown vegetables. Ornamental gardening was of secondary importance; however, my mother-in-law's Poulsen roses and the pansies were still a feature.

❧ ❧ ❧

Looking back, I realize Barnsley was a country-house garden typical of the 1930s, probably full of plants recommended by Gertrude Jekyll. The three-storey William and Mary house had been a rectory until 1932, when the parishes of Barnsley and Bibury were amalgamated and it was bought by my father-in-law, Cecil Henry Verey, on his retirement. Carved in stone over the garden door is the date 1697 with the initials 'B.B.'. These stand for Brereton Bourchier, squire of Barnsley, who built the house of

The north-west front of the house with its crumbling terraces; a photograph taken shortly after we moved here in 1951.

locally quarried Cotswold stone. Symmetrical, humble yet beautiful, it faces south-east and north-west, so has the full benefit of the rising and setting sun. Sadly, Bourchier's first wife died in childbirth in 1691 before the house was completed – you can see her marble memorial tablet above the altar in the north chapel of Barnsley church, and on the floor of the nave those of her firstborn twins, who died in January 1690. Bourchier remarried and went on to build the grander Barnsley Park on the northern outskirts of the village, and Barnsley House became the rectory.

❧ ❧ ❧

In about 1770 the Rev. Charles Coxwell built the high stone wall on three sides of the garden that still contains, protects and confines the property and is an essential element in the character of the garden. Then, as now, the wall ended in an elegant north-facing gothick survival summer house, probably built as an eye-catcher in a landscape style garden.

Richard Musgrave, younger brother of the squire, was rector in the 1830s; having been brought up at Barnsley Park, he found this rectory too small, so built an extension with a large cross-gable on the north-east end. You can still see the Musgrave coat of arms on the gable on the front façade of his new wing. The new porch, the verandah and the bow window were all given crenellations, and I like to feel that the finials above the gable were added at this time. The architect John Nash had been advising at the Park, so he might well have influenced the sympathetic gentrification of the rectory.

From 1841 Canon Ernest Howman was incumbent here for more than thirty years. We owe him a debt of gratitude for planting most of the fine trees that form the framework of the west and north sides of the garden today – limes, a Turkey oak, sycamore, beech and London planes. Between 1874 and 1900 the Rev. Daniel Compton was the incumbent. Then the Rev. Gerald Vidal took over. His daughters were famous for the delicious chocolates they made in the house. One of the Rectory girls, Margaret, was courted by an Australian airman stationed at nearby North Cerney airfield during the First World War, so impassioned that he dropped love notes wrapped in a calico sock on to the lawn from his aeroplane. He then captured his bride and carried her off to Australia.

His grandson, the celebrated art critic Robert Hughes, and his wife (now living in Shelter Island, New York) have been to Barnsley to see the trysting place and chocolate room.

❦ ❦ ❦

My father-in-law generously made the house over to his son in 1951. Here David and I lived together for thirty-three years – and then I lived alone there, until my son Charles inherited in 1988. My parents-in-law had moved into The Close, a converted stable block where I now live. They retained the small sheltered rectangular area which today is the temple and pool garden. We were to take care of the remaining three and a half acres inside the boundary wall.

When David and I moved into Barnsley House, in March 1951, we had already been thinking of it for several years as our eventual home, and by now I had acquired some measure of practical gardening experience. While David was away serving in the forces (with S.O.E., seconded from the Royal Fusiliers), I rented a cottage at Fairford. The three years I spent there were all-important in my gardening life. On Saturdays I was helped by Charlie Wall,

Cecil and Linda Verey, my parents-in-law, in the area that was to become the temple garden in the early 1960s, with the Rev. Charles Coxwell's wall behind.

a head gardener at nearby Quenington, from whom I learned how to sow seeds, grow vegetables, divide perennials and take chrysanthemum cuttings. He even taught me how to kill a duck. As in many cottage gardens there were treasures and excitements: a huge asparagus bed, an old apple tree, and best of all a shoulder-high lemon-scented verbena, *Aloysia triphylla*, happy in a sheltered corner. Half a century on I still love to have this plant.

David came home from the war and we lived at Ablington. Children – four of them by 1949 – and horses claimed more of my attention than gardening, but I was becoming aware of the garden and its seasons. I learned about the wonders of snowdrops in February, that auriculas have a beauty far surpassing the more humble primulas but equally demand more care and attention to give of their best. I learned a bit about soil, the importance of using plenty of organic material (we had manure from the ponies in the stables) and that dahlias will be killed by the first frost. In winter, I read avidly about vegetable growing and herbaceous borders; in spring and summer I then tried to implement this knowledge. I discovered that peas and beans, which flower and then fruit, have an annual life cycle like nasturtiums and marigolds, whereas delicious sprouting broccoli should be treated as a biennial, like sweet Williams and Canterbury bells. Root vegetables like carrots and parsnips resent being transplanted, so have to be sown in situ where they will develop in the same way as fennel and hollyhocks. All part of one's education in the garden, information like this is totally logical and soon becomes second nature.

So when we moved into Barnsley House, I had a sprinkling of gardening knowledge – how to sow, grow and propagate – but no idea about colour, form or design. I had always been interested in trees, so was immediately aware of the shelter belt that acts as an effective windbreak from the fierce west wind. There was a sycamore, a majestic Turkey oak, a copper beech, a sweet chestnut, yew trees allowed to luxuriate, and a mature chestnut (which has since fallen). Flanking the north side of the drive were two magnificent London planes, a chestnut that is a favourite with all the children as it produces top-quality conkers, and a lime that flowers prolifically in July for us to make lime-flavoured cordial. The scent of the flowers is incredibly sopo-rific and I can guarantee that my July visitors will oversleep and be apologetically late for breakfast (I know why!). There was also an acacia and a spreading yew. All these trees and the yews on either side of the pretty half-moon nineteenth-century entrance wall help not only to protect the garden from the icy winter winds but also to muffle the noise of the increasing traffic pounding through our village – a contrast to my first wartime visits here, when Mr Archer's milking cows went to and fro twice a day quite safely.

Rosemary and David Verey, 8 June 1940.

ଔଡ ଔଡ ଔଡ

The approach to Barnsley House is from the north-west. I learned from Russell Page that a driveway up which you pass quickly should have long sweeps of interest. Underplanting Canon Howman's trees we have a continuous carpet of yellow winter aconites for January and February, followed by blue scillas and species crocus. Then we fail: the trees come into leaf and nothing much will grow except the *Cotoneaster horizontalis* hiding the septic tank covers. Hellebores come and go and now, forty years on, I

am trying to establish *Symphytum grandiflorum*, which is supposed to grow anywhere. Garden planting inevitably changes and evolves.

The top of our drive, then as now, sweeps round the sentinel lime to bring you to the front door. On the right the lawn slopes, at first gently and then more steeply, taking you to the south side of the house and the flower garden. A western red cedar, *Thuja plicata*, stands beside a tall box tree, its branches sweeping gracefully and making an ideal hiding place for children.

Originally there were three terraces and retaining walls with borders in front, running the length of the house. In my mother-in-law's day filling the terrace borders was a major task twice yearly. Added to this they face north-west, so the plants lacked warmth and were always late coming into bloom. Colourful borders I thought looked out of place here. In 1961 the middle wall fell and we redesigned the terraces, making one 2.5-metre/8-foot high wall, a wider terrace and, in front, a low wall broken by central stone steps guarded by two stone animals – a whippet and a rather impressionistic sheep. Thus we tried to create straightforward simplicity and clear-cut lines, derived from stonework, trees and a well-mown lawn.

ଔଡ ଔଡ ଔଡ

On the south-west side of the house, dominated by the castellated verandah, the view of the garden is quite different today from when we took over in 1951. The lawn and the gothick summer house are there, but beyond were three yew hedges and herbaceous borders, with lawn between. The yew hedge on the right of the summer house, a boundary, remains; another, with its height reduced, has replaced an old lonicera hedge behind a nineteenth-century ilex; the third was turned to hide the swimming pool. We were amazed how successfully the yews transplanted: they were seventeen years old and head-high, but had made a dense network of small roots, which was no doubt their saving.

The borders on this side were very sparsely planted and later, when we changed it into the wilderness, I saw how poor and stony the soil here was. An early decision was to grass over the borders. Arthur Turner, the head gardener, had returned from war service to combat ground elder and bindweed. These were the days before Round-Up, and through a chance remark I discovered that if borders were sown with grass and mown regularly these weeds would ultimately die. So we did this, and it was remarkably successful. In doing so we created a large open space to fill with trees and shrubs of our own choosing within a framework of stone walls, mature trees and dense hedges.

The castellated verandah was added in 1830 and the terrace in 1960, before we made the knot.

My next step was not to hurry. In 1962, my son Charles made me a member of the Royal Horticultural Society and my daughter Davina gave me a large notebook immaculately covered with Florentine paper and importantly entitled 'Gardening Book' on the opening page. When I look back at my diaries I realize how some plants, treasured at the time, have disappeared, and I can appreciate how fast or slowly trees and shrubs have grown. Unless you date-tag trees as you plant them it is easy to forget how long ago it was – I could not remember when we planted the apple trees in the potager and started training them into goblet shapes, and I have just read in my diary that it was in March 1979. Also, when

we are putting a border to rights in the autumn, or searching for a shrub to fill a gap, I can look back for the names of plants I liked in the island beds at Wisley, or recall the June day when so many shrubs and trees were at their best in the Savill Garden, Windsor.

On the first pages of my book I took stock of our own garden, listing the trees and shrubs we had chosen in December 1961 for our wilderness area (see pages 132-143). In the rough grass among the daffodils we included specimens for spring blossom, berries and autumn colour, as well as for contrasting shapes and leaf texture. David was reminding me that I had grassed over many of his mother's borders and inquiring when I would turn my mind and energy to getting down to creating new borders. It was then that, without warning me, David invited the garden designer Percy Cane to come to Barnsley to give advice. This worried me, as I wished the garden to be our design and not someone else's, and it provoked me to action. This was the start of the parterre beds, the 'heart of the garden' (see pages 52-81). The horses were still important, so it became a divided loyalty. The main fact that I absorbed from this very brief professional visit was that you should include as many vistas as possible, using the longest distances, whatever the size of the site.

We soon put this into practice when we were siting the temple David was given from Fairford Park, which we erected in the pool garden (see pages 82-91). Then we became involved in creating our long vista, which eventually had the frog fountain as its focal point (pages 99-111 and 92-7). The narrow beds against the north-west-facing wall were filled with roses, clematis and shrubs that do

View of the house in about 1940 with Linda's perennial borders in the foreground – the area that was to become the wilderness.

best with some protection; wherever there was a space, annual climbers were added (see pages 112-9).

Patterns had become important to me, so first the knot garden and then the herb bed were laid out with geometric patterns (see pages 46-52 and 58). It was at about this time that I realized how exciting it would be to change the old vegetable garden into an ornamental potager (see pages 145-65).

Gradually the garden assumed its present layout, and when I moved into The Close I achieved my long-cherished wish to have a conservatory, built by my son-in-law, Hal Wynne-Jones (see pages 166-71). I still long for raised beds, a rose garden and some of the more unusual herbaceous plants. But by the time we have renewed the borders each year – digging, dividing, planting, feeding – and

looked after all the plants we are propagating, as well as coping with all the other routine tasks, there is little time left for working on a major new project.

❧ ❧ ❧

Although I arrived here more than fifty years ago, I constantly try to see the garden with new eyes. This is the wonderful thing about gardening: trees are ever growing taller, shrubs developing, ground cover taking over. The scene changes and every year has its own character, influenced by frost, rainfall and sunshine – elements over which we have no control; but we can aim to plan so that each season has its moments of interest, with winter scent, spring blossom and bulbs, summer exuberance and autumn colour.

The Way I See It

I never made a master plan of my garden. It has evolved slowly, probably because initially I knew little about design. Maybe this is the reason visitors say it is a restful garden, where they can relax and yet come upon unexpected corners. Some of the planting and features reflect the many influences I have had in my gardening life – from people, places and books. Thoughts crowd into my mind now, as they always do when I'm walking round the garden, remembering all the things my gardening friends and acquaintances have told me and all the garden scenes I have found inspiring. My notebooks remind me of some of them.

The 'Gardening Book' my daughter Davina gave me in 1962 no longer has immaculate covers but its pages are filled with ideas and impressions, a record of achievement and failure. Thirty years later I still keep intermittent diaries, and when I go round or read about an outstanding garden, I jot down the names of the more unusual plants, where they are growing and special associations. To note down events and impressions as they occur is tremendously helpful to beginners, such as I was in 1961, but it also serves to develop your memory as you yourself develop as a gardener.

❧ ❧ ❧

Knowledge of the art of gardening surely includes an appreciation of the history of design, of the movement of plants from one continent to the other, and of writings of both the ancients and contemporary authors. A turning point in my gardening life was when I started collecting old books. In the 1960s a friend of David's, a church historian, left me in his will a booklet called *The Mystic Mandrake*. Gradually I became aware of the importance of the classical Greek and Roman writers – Theophrastus, Dioscorides and Pliny – in the history of plants, and for the last thirty years it has been the greatest privilege to have on my shelves the earliest herbalists – William Turner, John Gerard and John Parkinson. Daniel Lloyd, the Kew bookseller, knew of my interest and found copies of the early horticultural writers for me – Thomas Hyll, Gervase Markham and William Lawson. Reading these sixteenth- and seventeenth-century books has given me an insight into Elizabethan and Stuart gardens that I could never have absorbed through reading only the interpretations of twentieth-century authors.

❧ ❧ ❧

As you learn about a subject every new experience means more to you and makes a long-lasting impression. I remember the gardeners and friends who were in my gardening life in the 1950s when I was becoming conscious of the importance of design and the choice of plants. Marjorie and John Buxton made me realize how important plant associations can be. Nancy Lindsay taught me to look at nature and made me more aware of beauty; her great advice was to use 'easy' plants when you start gardening and move on gradually to the more unusual and demanding plants. She also introduced me to hellebores for winter and spring, when you have time to appreciate them.

Some tips I learned from professional garden designers. Percy Cane explained the importance of long vistas in planning a garden – with us, that from the temple to the fountain. Peter Coats often visited at weekends, and he reiterated the importance of vertical as well as horizontal accents, especially in the potager. Russell

Page, another frequent visitor, stressed that simplicity is often best, a principle that shows in the elegance of his own work. Another of his wise remarks was that everything you put in the garden should be an addition, not a distraction.

❧ ❧ ❧

To my mind there is nothing to beat personal observation and visits to gardens. I remember particularly vivid periods when I seemed to encounter a rich number of new influences: 1972, for example, was a star year for me. My diary reminds me how I was discovering new plants, learning a bit more about design and certainly appreciating plant associations and colour combinations.

On Sunday, 16 April 1972 I went to Bampton Manor, Peggy Munster's garden. Peggy, a wonderful designer both in her house and her garden, had a perfect sense of colour and form. That day the woodland garden was a joy, with the deciduous trees all limbed up to allow in enough light for the swathes of wood anemones, dog-tooth violets, forget-me-nots, euphorbias, and daffodils in groups of one variety. Elsewhere, roses were carefully trained over iron 'shapes', hydrangeas promised well for late summer, and many viburnums and *Clematis armandii* were in flower. The circular herb garden had pink lavender alternating with Hidcote lavender and standard roses. David Vicary, who was with me, kept saying, 'Detail is all-important,' and here it was displayed perfectly.

At the end of April, we went to Devon and Cornwall, and here I learned the importance of scent. I decided we must have plenty in the garden – I like to have scented shrubs all through the year, especially in winter.

In June I paid a brief visit to the Oxford Botanical Garden, where I encountered some key plants. I noted *Salvia grahamii* grown right up the house wall, *Trachelospermum jasminoïdes* (the third time I had seen it that week!), *Veratrum viride*, *Geranium psilostemon*, *Maianthemum bifolium* and an enormous *Crambe cordifolia*. Now, many years later, I have achieved most of these, though the salvia is not hardy here outside.

A day or two later I went with my nephew Paul Sandilands to two gardens, both perfect but different. Caroline Somerset's cottage garden at Badminton, designed by Russell Page, has garden rooms, a beautiful rose garden glimpsed through old yew arches, lots of box edging and a potager with a French influence. At Barnsley I have tried to emulate the way in which the strong design of the garden is softened by an exuberance of planting. That same afternoon an even more lasting influence came into my gardening life. We went on to Alderley Grange, to Alvilde and Jim Lees-Milne's garden, which (to quote my diary): 'to my mind is a perfect garden – I do think Alvilde is a much better gardener than most of us. All is full and she has this feeling of joy of using every patch to capacity. It is a really happy experience for me in this garden: things are tutored, tidy, but not studied.' The lessons I have learned from Alvilde are many. Like Peggy Munster's, her garden was well structured and then filled with exuberant planting. I saw that if you get the shapes right, then your own love of plants will ensure a good garden.

My garden owes much to generous gardeners. In early July 1972 I brought home from Sally Westminster's garden at Wickwar cuttings of *Rosa* 'Cerise Bouquet'; these now form an effective screen between our vegetable garden and the lane. The *Itea ilicifolia* we have growing against our wall is also a cutting from Sally's garden. Keith Steadman, the willow expert, gave me a plant of his *Rosa* 'Wickwar' – a striking rambler flowering in July followed by a mass of orange hips. It is now a see-through screen between me and the main garden. Also that day I took home from Keith's nursery my original plant of *Ilex* × *altaclerensis* 'Lawsoniana', my favourite holly with three colours to its leaves.

An August visit to Professor and Mrs Hewer's garden at Henbury proved another horticultural lesson. Plants which I saw there and have since grown here were *Lysimachia clethroïdes*, *Sarcococca humilis*, *Hydrangea sargentiana*, *Teucrium* × *lucidrys* (a real stalwart), as well as *Aesculus parviflora*.

❧ ❧ ❧

Other sources of inspiration have been shows with their displays put on by some of the nurseries. I always looked forward to the Royal Horticultural Society shows at Vincent Square, especially those in the spring when many early bulbs were in flower. Seeing these plants growing rather than illustrated in a catalogue gives the true vision of how they look – of their colour and the plants they should be combined with. I especially remember Anthony Huxley taking care of me and guiding me round my first shows.

At one of these Tim Sherrard of Sherrard's Nursery had a stand with a bold display of *Iris histrioides*, at another a spectacular display of willows. Later I visited his nursery and brought home plants of *Salix hastata* 'Wehrhahnii' with silvery-grey catkins, *S. irrorata*, the young shoots covered with a white bloom, and *S.* 'Kuro-me' with black catkins. I aquired two other willows, one from Keith Steadman, *S. × rubra* 'Eugenei', with the earliest and most elegant small, pale mulberry catkins. It has given me as much February pleasure as any other plant in the garden. My other special willow is *S. daphnoides* 'Aglaia'. I took cuttings of this from Peter Birchall's garden at Cotswold Farm. These flourished and now every February I wait for the pale purple catkins to open, knowing that on a sunny day there will be flocks of honey bees from their home in the south-west gable of the house gathering the pollen from these early catkins.

❧ ❧ ❧

Over the last decade Hardy Amies has taught me that the eye of the perfectionist is all-important. He loves auriculas, old-fashioned roses and pelargoniums, clematis, box edging and plenty. I learned from Hardy that I must discipline myself. He once said of someone, 'Oh, she just wears clothes, she does not dress.' I translated this into a garden setting and immediately envisaged an overblown, blowzy border, plants carelessly put together with no colour scheme or firm structure. By contrast, the well-thought-out border – like the lady who 'dresses' – gives an immediate impression of satisfaction. It is all too easy to have a border looking bitty; I must aim at coordination. Just as the whole garden should have easy articulation, so the planting of the borders should flow.

I have clear pictures in my mind of both Christopher Lloyd's and David Hicks's gardens. Christopher must be the number one influence on the late twentieth-century generation of gardeners – a

brilliant plantsman, full of imaginative ideas. At Great Dixter in Sussex he inherited the care of a structured garden created by his parents and Sir Edwin Lutyens, and his genius lies in his ever-vital planting thoughts. He loves berries, shapes, skeletons mingled with evergreens and he helped me to realize that my garden is as important in winter as it is in June. His stimulating articles each week in *Country Life* constantly make us aware that adjacent colours which (I think) clash, should have a place in every garden. So now we have shell-pink *Oenothera speciosa* (the state flower of Texas) growing with orange eschscholzias from California. They both seed themselves where they flank a path and are contained within two lines of box edging only 30 centimetres/12 inches apart. Every time I walk along this path I think of him and remember that gardening must be fun.

I bow to David Hicks for his clearly defined theories. He has surrounded his house with a new garden of interrelated spaces dependent upon his instinctive eye for form. He has taught me the importance of using different mowing heights and of linking each space to create a natural flow and also a change of mood, sometimes simply relying on the infinite variety of the colour green.

Another influence on me has been Sir Roy Strong's garden in Herefordshire. In Elizabethan days and into the following century, symbolism was intensely important in garden planning. Every monument, pergola and alley had its meaning. As sophisticated visitors walked round the garden, their moods would change, influenced by the features they passed or saw in the distance. This was a spiritual emotion on an historical adventure. I sense this as I walk in Roy's garden, where he has used special features to commemorate certain events in his and his wife Julia's lives. From Roy I also learned to walk through my garden looking, questioning, imagining how a particular shape could be improved. It is so easy to become accustomed to a certain dullness in your own garden – you may need to shut your eyes and then open them again to change your vision and so your ideas.

Have gardens created and cared for by men had a different influence on me than women's gardens? I sometimes think so. Roy's and David's are definitely based on architectural structure, hedges, vistas and focal points. Great Dixter has both – flowers and structure. I have mentioned my visit to Alderley Grange in 1972, but I enjoyed and also learned much from Alvilde's last garden at Badminton. Structure was important to Alvilde, for she never forgot the French influence with clipped box and hollies. But she was in love with flowers and exuberant planting – wonderful roses, some as standards, others as climbers; the Mediterranean cistus and artemisias. She was never satisfied, always improving her border, and we should all remember to do this.

ᘏᕒ ᘏᕒ ᘏᕒ

Whenever I can do so, I visit gardens abroad, in Europe and in America. Often in recent years my diaries record gardens in the Pacific North-west, where we share a compatible climate. I also have many ideas from the planting of East-Coast gardens, where a strong formal design is important because of the difficult climate of hot summers and frozen winters. In the 1980s Peggy and David Rockefeller kindly invited us to see their garden in Maine, where the borders had originally been planned using annuals by the great American designer Beatrix Farrand. They were planted for spectacular displays from mid July to September. What stands out in my memory is the separate use of hot and cool colours. The 'cool' border, with penstemons, campanulas, delphiniums, violas, pansies creating a colour scheme of blues, greys, lilacs, pink and pale yellows, faces east, so it has the full benefit of the morning sun to give depth and delight. (I must always remember to consider the subtlety of the sun's rays when planning a garden.) The 'hot' border faces west, reminding us that bright colours show at their best in evening light with the slanting sun upon them.

ᘏᕒ ᘏᕒ ᘏᕒ

Years ago I was told, 'It is a sin to be dull.' Having met Bob Dash and basked in the originality of his garden in Long Island, I can comprehend this meaning. Bob has very clear-cut, artistic and original ideas about his gardens. He is primarily an artist and his garden is designed with a bravado which most of us lack. He also paints in bold swathes but plants with a delicate touch – our own

'Bob Dash' bed is my tribute to his planting style. His gates, doors and fences are in colours unusual in a garden, all geared to the appropriate season.

Ryan Gainey's garden in Atlanta, Georgia, has influenced my thoughts about planting. He has a rare vision, and like Bob, he is a genius at putting colours together and has taught me to look at small associations combined with broad effects. I think of both Bob's and Ryan's gardens through every season, but I had one memorable day in early spring in Delaware. Although a garden of many acres, Winterthur retains the feeling its creator intended – it is intimate. I spent a day with the late Hal Bruce when the *Adonis amurensis* and snowdrops were out and the hellebores just opening. Hal and I walked around, then dropped on to our knees to look into the hanging faces of the snowdrops. We found a galaxy of different species, and it was exciting getting our eyes attuned to the nuances of green markings and flower shapes. I left there knowing that I must look at plants closely and never neglect the touch of detail it is so easy to overlook.

We visited California in 1980. An inspiration at Filoli was seeing the way in which the olive trees had been shaped. The inside shoots are all pruned back, leaving a framework like a huge vase, allowing light into the centre. In fact, as Charles Webster, for many years President of the New York Horticultural Society, once said to me while walking through our wilderness at Barnsley, 'Rosemary, you must prune your trees so a bird can fly through them – then the light and air will get into them.' This is one of the most influential statements I carry in my mind as I spend happy hours in winter, shaping and tutoring our modest collection of trees.

David and I were taken to Muir Woods near San Francisco by Olive and George Waters, editor of the magazine Pacific Horticulture. Here we were filled with amazement by the size and majesty of the giant redwoods, so I felt very happy that we had chosen to plant a wellingtonia, *Sequoiadendron giganteum*, in our wilderness in 1966. No one should be deterred from planting trees which we may not live to see in maturity.

A visit to the Pacific North-west, driving along the coast and into the North Cascade Mountains with Steve Lorton, garden editor of Sunset Magazine, gave me a greater appreciation of the tall evergreen trees, the Douglas firs, and the long stretches of wild philadelphus growing by the streamsides in the mountains reminded me of Roberto Burle Marx and his style of planting in bold masses. The dry brown hills of the Yakima Reservation in Oregon, with their tawny look, reminded me of the brown stems and trunks of my winter shrubs and trees at Barnsley. It has taught me to think about the expansiveness of nature – that there must always be less tutored spots in my garden where we can let nature have its way, albeit keeping a gently controlling hand, as in our wilderness.

ↂ ↂ ↂ

Recently I was asked what my advice would be to a college student who was about to embark on a career in garden design. Not an easy question for me to answer, especially as my own garden knowledge and philosophy have been developed in different ways over many years, without professional training. Garden designing is an art form, even though it can be learned like any other subject by attending a course. Personal style is all-important. It is essential to spend time visiting gardens of various periods so you can discover how beds and borders evolve and change character over time and through the seasons. Take notes as you go; draw – even roughly – the shapes of trees and shrubs. Learn to build up your knowledge of plants, not only to be able to recognize them but to know what growing conditions they like or dislike, when they will flower, what their leaves will contribute before and after flowering, how they will relate to their neighbours. This knowledge comes only with familiarity, observation and experience.

Sometimes my notebook records an individual plant that stood out – like the *Aesculus parviflora* I first noted in 1962 growing at Stanton Harcourt in Oxfordshire. I first saw this shrubby member of the horse chestnut family in flower five years later. It was over 3.5 metres/12 feet high, leafy to the ground and covered with erect racemes of white candle flowers with pink stamens and red anthers. Seeing it was like meeting an old friend. I planted one at Barnsley, but in a sunless position where it did not thrive. Now

another has an important place in the car park, where it will get sunshine and appreciation.

Designing a garden, whether it is your own or a client's, involves drawing many threads together. When I am invited to help with the planning of a garden, I like first to walk slowly around the site, taking in where the warmest corners are likely to be, where the wind comes from, the view, the existing trees, the quality of the soil, any special features – in fact, getting a feel of the place. Then it is time to go into the house and look from all the windows – the kitchen, the dining room, the sitting room and, very important, the bedrooms. While doing this I can build up a picture in my mind of the owners' preferences. We discuss the colours and flowers they like, whether they will want water, or a place outside to sit on summer evenings. Do they entertain often, or have a young family? Will they work in the garden themselves and how will running it fit into their budget? I sometimes imagine that this is where I myself will live, so it must be a place that I will enjoy, but all the time I bear in mind that it is my clients' garden, individually designed for them, to suit their needs and their way of life.

ↂ ↂ ↂ

I like to take plenty of photographs to help me remember and to use when I'm trying out ideas, rather as Humphry Repton did with his 'before-and-after' sketches two centuries ago. A scaled ground plan with levels is essential, too. When I get home my first move will be to put a sheet of tracing paper over the ground plan and sketch in roughly where the paths and borders will be. The driveway is important and there should be a well-structured planting by the front door. This is where a border especially designed for winter interest can be good. During the long cold months it is pleasant for your visitors, and uplifting for you, to see coloured stems (cornus and willows), scented shrubs (witch hazel, winter sweet, *Viburnum farreri*) and a group of hellebores and snowdrops.

At this point I must curb myself and remember it is the overall plan which comes first, not the detailed planting. I think first about the hard landscaping – the walls or hedges, paths, borders and other key elements that create a firm structure. Once these bones are set out, the vistas become apparent; the paths become the arteries allowing circulation around the garden to bring it alive. Existing trees are incorporated into the plan, for a young garden needs all possible height and feeling of maturity. Year-round interest is essential and, to achieve this, evergreens make a vital contribution to the structure.

❧ ❧ ❧

I love the sheer variety of evergreen plant material with which you can shape garden spaces and vistas and punctuate your layout. Topiary can line a pathway, be an occasional feature, or make a statement by a front door or gateway. It may be a focal point, a living statue, a transition between garden rooms, or announce a change of mood. But it needs to be carefully sited, and must not be overstated – except in certain circumstances, as at Levens Hall in Cumbria or Ladew garden in Maryland, where it has become the major theme.

Moments of inspiration often come when you have been away and see your garden with new eyes on arriving home. When you look at something every day it is easy to take its appearance for granted, but a fresh perspective may suggest that you could improve a bush with a new look, maybe by taking off the lower branches, or trimming its head into a round. Yew and box are the specimens we think of as subjects for topiary, but faster-growing shrubs are ideal for quick effects. Golden privet, *Ligustrum ovalifolium* 'Aureum', and golden *Lonicera nitida* are both ideal for this. Nurseries often supply standards for sale – roses, the small-leaved lilac and hollies in many varieties, as well as *Euonymus fortunei* var. *radicans*.

Newly built brick or stone walls are a luxury, but over the years they are economical, for they need little maintenance – unlike growing hedges. They not only define a boundary but also provide protection from passers-by and prevailing winds, and a wonderful opportunity for growing climbing plants. If a wall is beyond the budget, then it is vital to decide where any windbreak hedges are needed, and to plant these without delay. Make sure that you or your contractor buy the best – smaller plants will often establish and grow on more quickly than taller specimens, which will

stand still for years before they put on new growth.

Yew has a reputation for growing slowly. I do not agree with this – time and impatience are relative. But if you want an established yew hedge, look for one which is to be uprooted and offer to remove it. Here are two golden rules for transplanting established shrubs: minimize the time they are out of the ground, and do not overload the root system with a disproportionate amount of top-growth. Yew will stand severe cutting back. It is better to have a lower well-furnished hedge that will grow on strongly than a taller, thinner one.

The trench for a new hedge planting must have a thorough soil preparation. Your hedge will be a permanent structure, so time spent on enriching the soil will be a future insurance. For a classic hedge, your choice can be yew, beech, hornbeam, box or a tapestry hedge with all these. A Saxon hedge, using only shrubs such as privet, box, holly, viburnum, roses and thorns which were growing in England a thousand years ago, is another idea.

❧ ❧ ❧

The variegated holly at the end of our beech hedge has now become a dominant feature, clipped into tiers with a ball at the top. Sir Roy Strong shaped this originally in the clever way he has with hedges and evergreens. Hedges are not merely divisions – they can be interesting features in themselves. At Barnsley David worked on the yew hedge which divides the lawn from the long border, copying the crenellations on the 1830s bow window and the verandah. They give the hedge an individual character and complement the gothick summer house. David also began shaping the two cones and an abstract shape above the yew hedge enclosing the swimming pool. Inspired by Roy, I realize that the top of an existing hedge, when shaped, gives a rhythm and breaks a too-dominant horizontal line.

Windows cut into hedges give another dimension and may be a vignette framing a distant feature. There are memorable yew hedges at Powis Castle on the Welsh border, now two hundred years old, battered, but beautiful; Christopher Lloyd's yew at Great Dixter was planted by his father, and the yew at Rodmarton Manor was planted in the 1920s. These are venerable examples, contributing great character, but we can all create peacocks in our own paradise, however small.

Box edging can define borders, fastigiate junipers and cupressus create height and patterns. At Barnsley we keep the old box bushes that I believe were planted in the 1840s trimmed to undulating shapes that suit the formality of the architecture of the house. Almost everywhere in our garden are neatly clipped box balls and pyramids, usually sited to define the beginning or the end of a border, and there are standard golden privet and *Euonymus alatus* edging an otherwise characterless stone path. The box edging forms an important part of the structure in the potager – we are always taking box cuttings so we have a constant supply of young plants to sell. Our original *Buxus sempervirens* 'Suffruticosa' hedge, probably a hundred years old, now growing under the espalier apples, came from a Cotswold garden where it had grown to a good 60 centimetres/24 inches high, very leggy and bare at its base. We bought it to Barnsley and planted it deeply and at an angle so the bare stems were covered. Now it is a foot-high edging, neat and very slow-growing.

Shapely deciduous trees, too, make a winter tracery of branches and add their own summer statement. When planning where to position trees, or the planting around existing specimens, it is important to weigh up the necessity of space. Beautifully shaped trees are worthy of their due measure of admiration – I think of the weeping cherry, *Prunus* × *yedoensis* 'Perpendens' (now *P.* × *y.* 'Shidare-yoshino'), and *Ulmus glabra* 'Camperdownii' – or they may have special seasonal qualities. A shrub such as *Aesculus parviflora* only reveals its wonderful shape and dramatic upright summer candles when in isolation, with enough space round it to allow it to be seen and admired from all sides.

❧ ❧ ❧

As well as their favourite plants, all designers have their strengths and special interests. Some are brilliant at making pools, others at finding the best plant combinations in the mixed borders, others at choosing interesting patterns in the layout or a strong structural framework and a general overall view with vistas, focal points, trelliswork and trees. For myself I particularly like well-planned paths. They may have a mundane purpose and destination, perhaps leading to the greenhouse or compost heap, or they may offer an invitation to meander. Winding paths can be narrow; they slow you down so you see as well as look. Straight paths wide enough to walk abreast lead you on more forcefully to a focal point. Retracing your steps does not matter: in doing so you will see plants and structure from a different angle and viewpoint.

If a client's garden is naturally flat, I wonder where and how a change of level can be created. A sunken garden using good brick or stonework for steps will probably be symmetrical and formal. I am thinking of the rose garden at Folly Farm in Berkshire, designed by Sir Edwin Lutyens and planted by Gertrude Jekyll, which you come on as a lovely surprise, entering between yew hedges and down beautifully built shallow steps. Pausing at the higher level before you descend, you can take in the pattern of the beds more clearly. In summer the carpet of roses and lavender below will waft their scent towards you.

If a sunken garden is impractical, consider a raised bed so that you can see the plants from a different viewpoint. Its retaining wall can be comfortable to sit on and gives the opportunity to use plants which love to cascade down, such as aubrieta, snow-on-the-mountain, *Parahebe perfoliata* and *Campanula portenschlagiana*, with their roots anchored in the bricks or stonework. A raised pool, as at Hidcote in Gloucestershire, brings the reflections nearer, and at this heightened level you can experience the feel of the water and get a closer view of the floating flowers. When a site is not level, well designed steps become an attractive feature in their own right, with a hand rail, balustrade or wall on each side to enhance comfort and appearance. Banks from one level to the next can have terraces whose retaining walls give opportunities for planting schemes.

Gertrude Jekyll wrote that a garden should curtsey to the house. A grand house must have a garden in scale and sympathy with it. Elizabethan houses are well complemented by an intricate series of gardens, the shapes of the beds often mirroring the plasterwork of the ceilings, the panelling, the brickwork or the outline of the gables. Three and four centuries ago there was not the diversity of plants we have today, and so patterned knot gardens and topiary, fountains and raised pathways called 'forthrights' – designed to give good viewing to the garden below – were all necessary design elements. Georgian houses, by contrast, need a landscape with sweeping views and parkland trees; the garden may 'leap the fence' with a ha-ha (as Horace Walpole said of William Kent's eighteenth-century designs), to make an uninterrupted view, a link between garden and grazing meadows. Victorian houses need detailed planting using colourful exotics, and modern architecture must have tree planting around it, as well as a lawn and mixed borders.

For Barnsley House, in its handsome William and Mary style, I have attempted to create a garden with strong bones, vistas, garden buildings, pleached walks, a wilderness and a potager, all to reflect the period. By my good fortune I have been able to make a garden with many moods but without defined garden rooms – this reflects my philosophy. I like to have a broad, sweeping view across the garden in winter when the herbaceous plants are low, a view that changes in summer as shrubs burst into leaf and the perennials stand tall.

❧ ❧ ❧

Just as the views from the windows of a house – my own or one whose garden I am designing – have always mattered to me, so do those from the various resting places. These give you time to pause and experience different reactions to what is around you. The lower eye-level of someone seated must always be considered when composing the surrounding planting.

Back in the 1950s, the most important viewing place for me was our bedroom window, the one above the drawing-room door. From there I could contemplate and plan. My in-laws' crazy paving path still runs directly from here across the garden towards the new iron gate in the old wall. On each side of the path eight sentinel Irish yews, planted in 1946, march in ordered discipline. They carry your eye to the gate and on to the focal point, a mature silver birch beyond the wall and the cow lane. I love this tree, which I chose from our then local nursery, John Jefferies of

Cirencester and Somerford Keynes. The young tree came bare-rooted and I selected it because of its promising white bark. It has different moods through the year. Bare of leaves and with a tracery of branches, the silhouette stands out in winter, both when the sky is blue and after a storm when there is a background of dark clouds; then the sun suddenly pierces through and highlights dramatically the birch's silvery trunk. In spring it never fails to produce a huge crop of catkins and, briefly, in autumn the leaves turn a soft parchment colour. We must keep it pruned and shaped so its shadow will not be cast too far across the potager.

Time passes and this same view, with the rock rose path between the yews, nowadays a major route for visitors, is no longer a solid ribbon of colour in May and June and has had a rethink. Turning recently to my diary of the 1980s, I found Russell Page's solution. He made me a rough sketch of narrow rectangular beds in the lawn between the yews, so years later, in early spring 1994, we got busy on these, marked out the beds and then planted them with a solid mass of rock roses and erodiums. It was amazing how by May the same year there was a carpet of colour – pink, carmine, bright red, orange, yellow – in a true Christopher Lloyd palette, startling but wonderful. Now, instead of a narrow path, you see a broader spectrum from the main house.

The path between the yews is an important avenue for the family as they walk into the garden from the house, but I do not think of it as the main vista. That one leads from the temple and pool garden to the fountain. Perfecting this vista presented us with problems. Often a project seems quite straightforward, and then when you come to carry it out difficulties reveal themselves. When we opened up the whole hundred-yard length of the view, the truth dawned on us that with the path at right angles to the temple, it was not parallel to the old wall, which had a 20-degree kink in it. Until you start measuring up, it is easy to be unaware of these oddities. From the temple, the lime walk planted parallel to the wall looked as though it were slipping away to the left. Compensation, I thought, was the answer, and I widened the path on both sides as it went towards the temple. This helped but was not the answer; the lime walk still seemed to slither away to the left. One day the late Nicholas Ridley, for many years MP for Tewkesbury and Gloucester (and grandson of Sir Edwin Lutyens), walked into the garden and solved the problem in a flash. His architectural talent made the solution obvious – plant another row of limes. It worked wonders, and to complete the picture the border we call the 'Bob Dash' bed was added beside the laburnum and the edges of the borders on the other side had to be adjusted.

The rock rose path and the temple vista are the two most important throughout the year, but other axes are significant at particular times or make subtler statements. The strongest is the lime walk leading on into the laburnum tunnel. Then parallel to this and the wall is the winter walk, where a rickety brick path leads to a walnut tree. (After the path was laid, moles moved in and hummocked its surface.) As you wander along you can pause awhile on my son Charles's seats. One view leads between the mixed borders towards the grey cedar, *Cedrus libani* ssp. *atlantica* Glauca Group, planted in the winter of 1939. Another has a subtle glimpse through the yew hedge towards the stone hunting lady carved for us by Simon Verity. The potager has its own smaller vistas too, but you will find these as you walk among the vegetables.

I think about the vistas of my own garden when designing for other people. If the garden is long and narrow, a straight path down the middle is too obvious. The length can be broken by hedges or trellis, with cross-vistas within them. This theme can be worked on to define different areas, each given its own character, using planting to create the colour scheme and mood: one part laid aside for children, another for a pond with scented plants and, very important, a quiet place to sit.

In larger, square or rectangular gardens there will be a main vista or perhaps an avenue, and, as at Barnsley, subsidiary, less dominant sight-lines will emerge as the plan evolves. Working in an existing garden it can sometimes be difficult to superimpose straight lines and the shape of beds may have to be altered. I do like symmetry, but this should be flexible. A golden rule, taught by Beatrix Farrand, is never to bend the site to suit your plan – your plan must fit the site.

The late Lord Buchan's garden in Bourton-on-the-Water was one I loved to visit; it gave me many ideas. One day when he was walking round my garden he said, 'I do like the way you make vistas into the borders.' It took me a moment to understand his meaning, then I realized it was the fact that we often put taller plants in front and allow a view through to lower ones at the back. I have attempted to repeat this all through our borders and in my planting plans for my clients.

Remember, on the other hand, not to obscure an existing view or detract from it by too much detailed planting. A fine view can be emphasized with subtle planting or by framing it with an arch. An example which I remember is in the late Mrs Lockwood de Forest's garden in Santa Barbara. She had planted a belt of trees for protection, but had left a gap so that when sitting on her lawn in the evening the highest mountain in the distance and the setting sun were framed by the trees.

❧ ❧ ❧

Ornamental features such as statues, pots and containers add so much to the garden, and plenty of thought should be given to these. Statues must be searched for or commissioned and will have a permanent site, with the right planting around and framing them. If a statue forms the focal point of a vista, it must be of the right scale. The fun of pots and containers is that they can be moved around. They can have seasonal planting, changing for summer and winter, or a permanent evergreen feature. On a practical note, your containers need to be close to a water supply.

I believe that people should think more carefully about their gates and garden furniture. Gates can be so original and attractive – design your own and have them made up. Colour is important, as it is with garden furniture. Natural wood is often the best, but if you favour colour then do be imaginative. Use dark blue or dark green, or a pale colour to suit the situation; white is usually too intrusive. If you cannot find the exact shade you want on the paint chart, do not be afraid of mixing your own. Well-made garden furniture is essential: it will look better and last longer than the plastic stuff you pick up.

My thoughts and impressions have developed continuously

through seeing great gardens or small ones where ever I found a vignette of beauty, in Europe and in America. Certain days and stays, visiting in American gardens, have had a lasting effect on me, encouraging me to be more adventurous. On the east coast in Delaware, Bill Frederick's way of planting, reminiscent of Roberto Burle Marx's work, in grand sweeps along the hillsides round his house are memorable to me. Bob Dash's Long Island garden has taught me not to be afraid of using colour on gates and fences – I have recently painted a solid wooden door set in a stone wall a cardinal red. Charlie and Chuck Gale of Pennsylvania have inspired me to use mature specimens in strategic positions. Ryan Gainey's inspiration has been never to be dull, planting for all seasons so that one merges with interest into the next.

Three special friends whose ideas have helped to stimulate my own are the garden designers Tim Rees, John Hill and Rupert Golby. I have worked with all of them on various gardens and we have all contributed our thoughts. It is important to be receptive to ideas, both artistic and practical, and wherever possible to listen to gardeners who have a fund of knowledge.

⊶ ⊶ ⊶

All these thoughts have influenced me – almost subconsciously – in my own designing. My aim is to remember that plants love to know they are being cared for and given the situation they like best. I like to plant in layers, with tulips and narcissus coming through early bulbs. The leaves of herbaceous plants such as hostas, ferns or delphiniums hide the untidy leaves and bulbs.

We must all examine our environment, always gaining inspiration from existing natural features; we will then enhance rather than overwhelm our surroundings. I always hope that my clients' knowledge and involvement with their gardens will increase every year. Then I hope they can appreciate what I have done for them initially and the garden will truly be theirs. I hope to be invited back to see what they have contributed to my original plans. Some clients are more appreciative than others, and I feel complimented when they ring me and say, 'Do come and see your garden'. I will.

The Garden Tour

1 The Driveway
2 The Front Terrace
3 Way in from the Car Park
4 The Terraces
5 The Verandah
6 The Knot Garden
7 Parterre Bed No. 1
8 The Herb Garden
9 Parterre Bed No. 2
10 Parterre Bed No. 3
11 Parterre Bed No. 4
12 The Yew Walk
13 The Temple and Pool Garden
14 The Frog Fountain and Border
15 The Ribbon Beds
16 The Lime Walk
17 The Laburnum Walk
18 The Winter Walk
19 The Grass Walk
20 The 'Bob Dash' Bed
21 The Walls
22 The Broad Border
23 The Gothick Summer House
24 The Croquet Lawn
25 The Wilderness
26 The Swimming Pool
27 The Hunting Lady
28 The Cow Lane
29 The Silver Birch
30 The Tennis Court
31 The Potager
32 The Old Cow Shed
33 The Courtyard
34 The Conservatory
35 The Selling Yard

Note: Planting plans for each area of the garden are based on the year 1994.

N

Evergreens

Evergreen trees and shrubs are important in the structure of the garden all through the year, but in winter, when the deciduous trees are bare and herbaceous stems cut down, they play the leading role. Clipped, they take on the form you choose (**left**). Here, in the herb bed, the stage is set: the diamond shapes of the box stand out clearly when the herbs are low and frost has painted their flat surface silver. Making a vertical contrast, the 1-metre/3-foot-tall box cones mark the four corners of this bed. Beyond, the upright Irish junipers, the main vertical accent, have an important role.

The evergreen oak, *Quercus ilex*, and the beech and yew hedges frame the gothick summer house as you look along the path (**right**). The Rugosa rose hedge has come into leaf even before the beech has shed its leaves; creamy-white narcissus bloom underneath. To mark the end of the hedge is a variegated holly, clipped into tiers, with pale half-hidden primroses at its base. I love the look and rustle of brown beech leaves in winter, but it seems unnatural that they do not fall before the fresh green leaves of other shrubs open. Is the beech dead, one wonders? *Euphorbia characias*, golden feverfew and ferns have seeded themselves between the stone steps into the summer house.

Horizontals and verticals

Strong horizontal lines run across this picture (**right**): the rugosa rose hedge, the beech hedge – looking alive once more with its new foliage – and the top of the lime trees. Three rounded shapes are important, too: the *Berberis* × *ottawensis*, a weeping crab, *Prunus* 'Red Sentinel', and the dome of the topmost tier of the variegated holly. Lily-flowered *Tulipa* 'Mariette' brighten the box-edged squares under the crab-apple, the multi-stemmed acer and the bare mulberry, which waits to spring into leaf when danger of frost is past.

In summer the tall dark junipers, still dominant in form and height, contrast with the rounded tree lupin and its yellow flowers (**left**). The delphiniums on the left will grow taller as they open more fully. In the foreground the pink flowers of *Lamium maculatum* clash with the orange-red of *Euphorbia griffithii* 'Fireglow'. This euphorbia is a spreader and so is the *Phlomis russeliana*, a good plant for its skeleton of seed heads in winter. On the right the new growth on *Juniperus* × *media* 'Pfitzeriana' glows yellow too, and its spreading branches create a spot for shade-loving plants.

The yew walk and views across the knot

In late May and early June the rock rose path, lined each side with upright Florence Court yews, *Taxus baccata* 'Fastigiata' (**left**), leads your eye through the blue iron gate and beyond to the white trunk of the silver birch by the potager, seen in winter (**right**). The rainbow-coloured helianthemums have taken precedence along this path for twenty-five years. Grown first from seed sown direct into ever-increasing cracks between the paving stones, we now replace any casualties and woody specimens to keep a continuous bright ribbon (**below**). In the foreground magenta-red hardy geraniums have self sown from those in Bed No. 1. A double orange Welsh poppy nestles under one of the yews.

Views across the knot in winter and summer (**following pages**). Morning sun adds drama to this snowy view, highlighting every nuance (**page 30**). Looking over the knot's undulating threads across the main lawn towards the gothick summer house, every tree and shrub has its snow cover: the fat hollies, the Rugosa rose hedge, the old evergreen oak and the beech, its lower branches hanging down with the weight of the snow. On its left and behind the yew hedge, the chestnut tree glistens.

Looking across an edge of Bed No. 2 to the knot garden and sundial, and over the main lawn to the sunlit hunting lady framed by an old box 'tree' and the evergreen *Viburnum rhytidophyllum* (**page 31**). Golden hop, *Humulus lupulus* 'Aureus', weaves its way up and over the box in summer. In the foreground border are *Cosmos* 'Sensation', aruncus, *Salvia nemorosa* 'Ostfriesland', *Aster × frikartii* and pink penstemons.

Views through the heart of the garden

The Tuscan temple viewed through Bed No. 4 (**left, above**). In the foregound the bright *Geranium psilostemon* stands out well in colour and contrast to the dark purple-blue delphiniums backed by *Rhamnus alaternus* 'Argenteovariegatus'. *Rosa* 'Penelope' has climbed through and flowers above the rhamnus. Painted iron gates and *Clematis* × *durandii* provide more blue in this border of mixed colours. The new growth on the horizontal *Juniperus* × *media* 'Pfitzeriana' adds a touch of gold.

The Simon Verity sculpture of my lady gardener (**left, below**) draws the eye to the wall, the blue gate and the ivy, so that here (Bed No. 4) streaks of blue delphinium, spots of magenta geranium, orange alstroemeria, puffs of *Campanula lactiflora* and the bold brush stroke of juniper become a living Impressionist painting.

In late May aquilegias, from darkest purple to soft pink, weave their way between *Euphorbia characias*, orange Welsh poppies and penstemons (**right**) in Bed No. 2. The philadelphus gives a background and windbreak; seen over these, the mellowing pillars of the verandah and the clipped holly add shape and structure.

Tree shapes and branches for winter interest

A pair of weeping cherries, *Prunus × yedoenis* 'Shidare-yoshino', stand each side of the rock rose path. Planted here as an entrance to the lime walk and a full stop to the yew walk, their strong, symmetrical weeping shape, with branches sweeping to the ground, makes a see-through curtain in winter. We cut out any too-vigorous branches to prevent them spreading or they would hang both ways over the paths. Behind the one shown here (**left**) the upright red winter twigs of *Tilia platyphyllos* 'Rubra' contrast with the cherry in habit and colour. An old walnut, planted years before David and I came to Barnsley, has a beautiful tracery of branches, some spreading horizontally and others stretching upwards. Every garden should have a walnut to enjoy in winter and, recently, my son Charles chose two walnuts for the wilderness.

The winter look of the silver birch (**right**) is different again – more delicate and airy than the walnut, as silver-trunked as the red twigs of the lime, and in its tracery of branches as delicate and wind-blown as the cherry's are firm and determined. On blue-sky days in winter and when the sky is overcast with dark clouds, this tree is always beautiful, standing out against its background. In this evening light the trees of the ancient hedgerow bounding the ridge-and-furrow field have an exciting rose-tinted look. The field has not been ploughed for centuries, since medieval times, and the hedge has at least seven different species – oak, ash, hawthorn, spindle, blackberry, wild rose and wayfaring bush. At one time, no doubt, it was cut and laid, but we leave it to be as the Saxons knew it.

The path curves to the left, leading you into the potager.

Statuary and garden ornaments

Statuary and ornaments must be as carefully placed as seats in the garden – they can be moved until the perfect place is found for them. Which should come first, the site or the statue? Either can, I think.

The style of our one-time neighbour

Simon Verity has changed over the years. He knows our garden well, and between the 1970s when he carved the hunting lady and designed the frog fountain, he has made us the stone pyramids and our two atmospheric gardeners. The gardeners, bought in 1982,

first stood by the wooden gate into the potager. David moved them after a year to their present home in the flower garden, where they stand either side of the blue iron gate in the wall, leading to the cow lane. They have a very eighteenth-century Italian look, Simon having recently travelled in Tuscany. The lady, with her pale complexion and moss ornament (**opposite, left**) holds a cornucopia of flowers, and her companion

(**opposite, right**), who clearly cares for his potager, carries a selection of fruit. Notice every detail of these figures: her beads and his basket and apron.

We chose the pyramids (**above, left**) from Simon's workshop. They make just the right invitation to stroll along the brick path through the box-ball-lined winter walk. This brick pathway is one of the three walks taking you from the temple garden to the

south-west boundary wall.

The solid stone urns standing each side of the elegant bull-nosed stone steps (**above, right**) could have been here since 1697, when the house was built and this was the front door. Their permanence is emphasized by their wonderful patina of gold and silver lichen. The old clay pots are easily moved and reflect the season. Two *Francoa ramosa* are a late summer and autumn choice.

Strategic seats

Seats at strategic places round the garden provide an opportunity to sit and consider, plan some future planting, or look critically at a tree or shrub and wonder how to prune it and improve its shape.

A favourite place to sit, especially in June when the laburnum and wisteria are in flower (**above, left**). The chair, a Chinese Chippendale prototype made by my son Charles in 1982, is sturdy and comfortable.

Sitting here, you look under the branches of two pleached limes towards the first section of the broad border. There is a feeling of privacy, it is out of the wind, and the trees cast just enough shade on hot days. Placing seats is as important as siting your trees, so move them around until you are satisfied they allow the best view. On your left as you sit are Simon Verity's stone pyramids, *Allium aflatunense*, dark purple aquilegias, tansy leaves, euphorbia in flower and variegated euonymus on the wall.

The arbour in the potager (**above, right**)

faces south-east. Its seat, called the Napoleon armchair, was also designed by Charles. The leaves of the vine, *Vitis* 'Brant', colour to a warm orange as the grapes ripen in autumn. Bay bushes flank the arbour, *Helleborus foetidus* has seeded, and a leek has been left to make decorative seed heads.

Seats in the garden in winter are more for adornment than for use, except on the rare balmy winter day. This metal seat under the evergreen oak (**right**), a Winterthur Museum reproduction, looks towards the south-west façade of the house.

The Terraces
and Verandah

As you go through the archway from the selling yard – don't be tempted to linger there on your arrival – the garden comes upon you as a surprise. Pause awhile, between the yews, and allow yourself time to study the structure of the garden. Enjoy the façade of the house. In summer the sun lights up the beautiful patina of the Cotswold stone from dawn until after midday; the afternoon sun warms the 1830s verandah and laters pours through the windows of the north-west front. Now turn to explore the planting.

❧ ❧ ❧

Go down the stone steps and immediately turn right along the narrow path that leads you beside the herb beds to what was my old kitchen door – now the entrance to my daughter-in-law's antiques shop – and a display of my son's garden furniture. The old Victorian greenhouse, now sited in the selling yard, occupied this corner when we moved here in 1951. At that time Hiram Winterbotham, who had a garden at Woodchester in Gloucestershire, was a strong influence on our gardening life. He was a born teacher and to walk with him round his garden was a horticultural inspiration. His great interest was trees and shrubs allowed to grow naturally, often twining into each other and acting as supports for honeysuckles, roses and clematis.

Because of Hiram, my instinct when choosing shrubs to clothe the house has always been to select climbers with a scent. To the right of the door, planted in the 1950s, is *Rosa mulliganii* (often mistaken for *R. longicuspis*), which bears its large clusters of fragrant white flowers in early July. This rambler is a rampant climber, very attractive to bumble bees as well as honey bees.

On the other side of the door an old wisteria had sent up a single trunk to the roof, but never flowered. My first gardener, Arthur Turner, assured me that it was growing in such meagre soil that it would never oblige. Luckily, I went to a brilliant series of lectures on pruning at the Royal Horticultural Society's garden at Wisley. After an initial brave removal of the dominant trunk, to allow the subsidiary branches to develop and be trained horizontally as well as vertically until a framework was established, we started a routine twice-yearly pruning. In July and in the autumn the long arms of new growth are clipped tidily back to two or three buds which will develop into flower trusses. It has a spring share of manure and now flowers abundantly.

Planted beside the wisteria is a *Clematis cirrhosa* var. *balearica* given to me by Caroline Burgess. It is amazing, twining through the wisteria and in mild winters blooming non-stop from December through to March. The flowers are creamy-white with reddish-purple speckles. It is now right up to the roof, and another visit to Wisley may be necessary for advice to discover how much I can cut it back. The underplanting is a clump of *Iris unguicularis*, rosemary, self-sown *Corydalis lutea* and pots of useful herbs.

❧ ❧ ❧

The steps here lead down to the cellar and we have concealed them with evergreen shrubs, all planted years ago in a stone trough 3.5 metres/11½ feet long by only 25 centimetres/10 inches wide and deep. There is an upright juniper, variegated box and *Lonicera nitida* 'Baggesen's Gold'. How these have survived, growing in so little soil, is a mystery, especially as *Cotoneaster horizontalis* and ivies

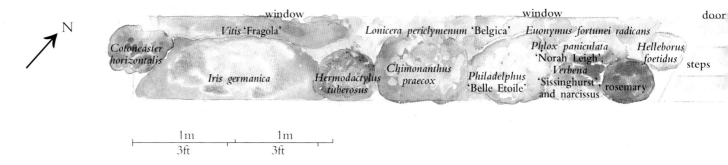

have crept in to join them. Another offering by the cellar steps is a *Hebe speciosa*, which at least twenty years ago seeded itself into the paving and flowers in profusion in July.

❧ ❧ ❧

An evergreen *Phillyrea angustifolia* now puts on too much growth every year for its situation and has to be constrained from taking light from the windows. Stretching under the windows and up and over the phillyrea is a 3-metre/10-foot tall well-scented *Lonicera rupicola* var. *syringantha*. This unusual shrubby honeysuckle has small pink flowers appearing first in May and then again, but more gently, in autumn. I have put *Berberis thunbergii* 'Rose Glow' in front to pick up the pink of the honeysuckle. In this same small bed are two clematis, a weeping rosemary, and another favourite – the thornless *Rosa* 'Zéphirine Drouhin', growing by the drawing room steps. It must be the oldest inhabitant, for a photograph taken in 1899 of the Rev. Daniel Compton and his family posed on the steps shows 'Zéphirine Drouhin' in full flower.

Framing the same doorway a *Euonymus fortunei* var. *radicans* – with no scent – planted in the 1950s, has managed to climb up and around the bedroom windows. It shares its position with the early Dutch honeysuckle, *Lonicera periclymenum* 'Belgica', which has a wonderful scent as it drifts into the bedrooms in late May. *Philadelphus* 'Belle Etoile', below the window, is generous with its white flowers, which open at the end of June. This is an indispensable shrub for the garden and good for flower arranging, but you should allow time to remove the leaves when you use it indoors.

A wintersweet, *Chimonanthus praecox*, now thirty-five years old,

flowers profusely from December through to January or February. Its strong honey-fragrance wafts around the terrace on the winter air. The old lady who gave it as a small specimen to David in the 1950s warned him, 'It may not flower for seven years, but you will never regret waiting for its scent.' She was right and our patience has been well-rewarded, but a point we did not appreciate was the size it would grow to: it has now scaled the house wall. Once the flowers are over it is shaped to prevent it from darkening the window of the drawing room.

❧ ❧ ❧

As you round the corner, you reach the verandah, added in the 1830s, which shelters the *Vitis vinifera* 'Fragola', called the strawberry vine by Vita Sackville-West. The many bunches of small grapes ripen in October and make delicious jelly. The four ornamental terracotta pots on the verandah we brought home from Italy in 1970. In winter they are planted with specimen hollies and box, surrounded by species crocus, narcissus and tulips; in summer, scented-leaved pelargoniums are used with *Helichrysum petiolare* and the ever-blooming *Bidens ferulifolia*.

A *Leycesteria formosa* has seeded into the paving, *Daphne odora* 'Aureomarginata' flowers here in March, and *Buddleja davidii* 'Dartmoor' in late summer. Unfortunately, a bush form of elm – *Ulmus × hollandica* 'Jacqueline Hillier' – is slowly becoming a tree. To round off the corner and the picture is a great box bush, planted I think in 1830 and now an elegant, venerable mass. Established with it is an old bay tree. Both the box and the bay keep the wind away from the knot garden and the sitting-out terrace.

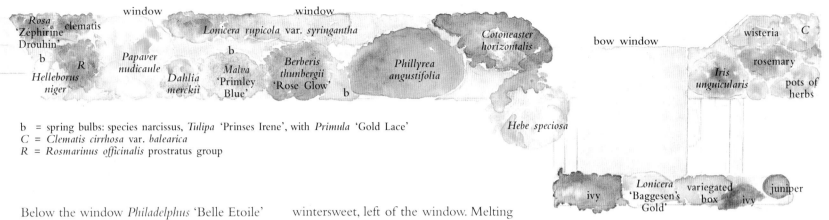

window   window

Rosa 'Zephirine Drouhin'   clematis

Lonicera rupicola var. *syringantha*

b

Papaver nudicaule

b
R

Helleborus niger

Dahlia merckii

Malva 'Primley Blue'

Berberis thunbergii 'Rose Glow'

b

Phillyrea angustifolia

Cotoneaster horizontalis

bow window

Iris unguicularis

wisteria   C

rosemary

pots of herbs

Hebe speciosa

ivy

Lonicera 'Baggesen's Gold'

variegated box

ivy

juniper

b = spring bulbs: species narcissus, *Tulipa* 'Prinses Irene', with *Primula* 'Gold Lace'
C = *Clematis cirrhosa* var. *balearica*
R = *Rosmarinus officinalis* prostratus group

Below the window *Philadelphus* 'Belle Etoile' (**below, left**), with *Euonymus fortunei radicans* to the right and *Chimonanthus praecox*, wintersweet, left of the window. Melting snow clings to *Daphne odora* 'Aureomarginata' (**below, right**).

Seasonal containers

Three close-up plantings on the verandah (general view, page 40). We brought the decorative clay pots home with us from Orvieto in Tuscany in 1972. They stand on the verandah all year long and have never suffered any frost damage. In winter either box or holly is a central feature, and we surround these with thickly planted bulbs – species crocus to open on sunny days in February (**below**), followed by narcissus, choosing a different variety each year. These are a split-corona variety (**opposite, left**). We add a few 'Paper Whites' each year for

scent and they often surprise us by flowering around Christmas time. To take care of colour in April and May there are *Tulipa* 'Fancy Frills'; their colour goes well with the Cotswold stone. *Leycesteria formosa*, on the left of the pots, has seeded itself between the paving and steps.

After the bulbs are taken out the summer display varies each

year. Here (**opposite, right**) golden and grey forms of *Helichrysum petiolare* support South African *Bidens ferulifolium*, which flower non-stop until late autumn, when their place is taken by our cycle of bulbs and central evergreen. Long shoots of the strawberry vine, *Vitis vinifera* 'Fragola', twirl over the *Cotoneaster horizontalis*.

box

bay

Daphne odora 'Aureomarginata'

Ulmus × hollandica 'Jaqueline Hillier'

Lonicera pileata

Solanum jasminoïdes 'Album'

Rosa 'Danse du Feu'

Clematis 'Nelly Moser'

N

1m
3ft

window

p = pots
winter: box, holly, crocus, narcissus, tulips
summer: *Helichrysum petiolare* 'Limelight' and *Bidens ferulifolia*

window

Leycesteria formosa

verandah

Cotoneaster horizontalis

Vitis vinifera 'Fragola'

The Knot Garden

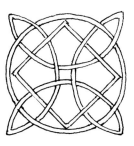

When this house was built in 1697, formal gardens were still the fashion in England, so historically it was appropriate to give the garden a basic formal design. We had already made the four parterre beds in the 1960s, but by 1970 – after studying Elizabethan and seventeenth-century knots for the Garden History Society – I felt compelled to make a knot garden at Barnsley.

In my library I had Gervase Markham's *The Countrie Farm* (his 1616 translation of Estienne and Liébault's *La Maison Rustique*) and *The Compleat Gardeners Practice* by Stephen Blake (1664). Knot gardens were often complex, but I found one in each of these books that could be copied on a small scale. There was only one obvious place to position them – on the south-west side of the house, overlooked by the verandah. A photograph of about 1900 shows a formal rose garden in exactly this position. We planted the knots side by side between the old box hedge and one of the parterre beds (Bed No. 2); their size – each five yards (metres) square, with a yard surround – was dictated by the space available.

❧ ❧ ❧

I followed Gervase Markham's advice: first make your design on paper and then superimpose grid lines. Using cord and pegs, stretch out this grid on the ground and copy the knot over it with a trail of dry sand. Meanwhile, I had collected enough plants to create the interlacing threads – two varieties of dwarf box, *Buxus sempervirens* 'Suffruticosa' and *B.s.* 'Aurea Marginata', as well as wall germander, *Teucrium × lucidrys*.

Markham recommended filling the spaces between the threads with coloured earths. The colours were those traditionally used in heraldry: Flanders tiles ground finely for red, sand for gold, coal dust for black, chalk for silver, and coal and chalk mixed for blue. We kept the five colours for some time, but they were not always easy to obtain, and to keep the pattern looking fresh they had to be renewed at least once a year. Eventually we became content with our local gravel.

The knots themselves are the picture; their 'mount' is now an enclosing strip of gravel. The frame was originally a low rosemary hedge, but this was killed one severe winter, so we resorted to hardier box. When I saw the knot garden at Filoli in California in 1980, I realized that the interlacing 'threads' had been clipped to give the impression that they go over and under one another. I had never seen this done in England, so on coming home we got busy with clippers and started to shape the intersections of our knots to convey this impression. The patterns were immediately given new life and a rhythm of which I feel sure the Elizabethans were aware, although I have never found it conveyed in old books.

Once established these undulations are easy to keep shaped, but clipping at the right time is essential to maintain a fresh and well-tutored look. We wait until most of the new growth is developed, which – depending on the season – is at the end of May or in early June, when we do the major trim using hand clippers. In August it will need another tidy, but this time there will be only a few stray and straggling young shoots to trim.

At each of the four corners of this double knot, overlooking the scene, stands a dramatic holly, *Ilex × altaclerensis* 'Golden King', shaped into two circular tiers. I realize how lucky it is that these hollies (given to me in the 1970s by Mr Mitchell, head gardener at Bruern Abbey) are variegated: dark green would be too heavy and pure gold too strong above the low pattern of the knot.

We were fortunate in another way. When I was planning the knots, I had not fully appreciated how much time the clipping takes at a busy moment of the year. Early in June Andy, who is responsible for tending our knot garden, is also mowing and planting peas, beans and lettuce in the potager as well as clipping all the other box bushes around the garden, and can only afford to spend two days in this area. The whole beauty of the knots depends on how well tutored the box is kept, and I am thankful that we chose to place them where we did, in a space that restricted their size. As Humphry Repton recommended two centuries ago, any planting close to a house helps to keep it 'anchored' into its surroundings. Our knots have become almost a shadow of the house.

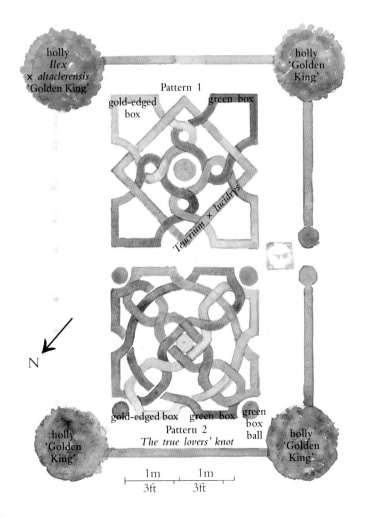

holly *Ilex* × *altaclerensis* 'Golden King'

holly 'Golden King'

Pattern 1

gold-edged box

green box

Teucrium × *lucidrys*

N

holly 'Golden King'

holly 'Golden King'

gold-edged box   green box   green box ball

Pattern 2
The true lovers' knot

1m / 3ft   1m / 3ft

Topiary

The knot garden in early spring (**right**), with *Helleborus orientalis* and narcissus in the nearby border. Strong vertical accents – the sundial, the hunting lady statue in the distance and the four hollies – stand out in contrast to the horizontal layout of the knot and the low rounded shape of one of its centrepieces and round box shapes behind. The evening sun, catching the foliage, casts interesting patterns and makes the garden glow.

Looking across the knots (**previous page**) towards the parterre beds in midsummer. In the foreground is 'The True Lover's Knot', taken from Stephen Blake's *The Compleat Gardeners Practice*. Beyond is the design taken from Gervase Markham. The evening sun lights up the interlacing box threads giving the pattern an interesting rhythm. The double tiers of 'Golden King' hollies stand guard at the corners.

The Heart
of the Garden

As you walk out of the drawing room door, down the elegant stone steps flanked by solid old urns, the crazy paving path creates an important vista. You may wonder which way to walk – will it be along this path between the yews, or will you branch out across the lawn to wander round and enjoy the parterre beds?

Garden visitors, however, having approached through the archway from the sales yard, will most likely look to their right, attracted by the architecture and mellow stone of the house. They will pass the herb border, put conveniently near the door David had made leading to my old kitchen. When I created this feature in the 1970s, I was influenced by my memory of two herb gardens I had seen many years before. One was in a garden at Fairford and the other had been made by John and Marjorie Buxton at Cole Park near Malmesbury. Both had patterns of diamonds and triangles, created by low box threads and infilled with herbs, and I copied this theme. In a cottage garden it is traditional for herbs to be intermingled with annuals, perennials, bulbs and roses, but I decided at Barnsley I would keep my kitchen and stillroom herbs, particularly those grown in Elizabethan times, in the patterned bed by my new door. The overall shape was dictated by geometry and the space available. It provided a link between our parterre beds and the house, looked decorative as well as functional – and I loved having it so close to the kitchen. Its firm structure stands out in winter and overflows with herbs in summer. The various compartments are filled with culinary herbs such as thyme, mint, marjoram, purple and grey sage, chervil, dill, chives, sorrel and parsley. One triangle has *Artemisia abrotanum*, recommended in the sixteenth and seventeenth centuries for putting into the clothes closet and linen press to keep away moths. There is Egyptian onion, useful when only a hint of flavour is wanted in the salad, and camomile to infuse as a tea. Visitors are always interested in the single plant of *Iris* 'Florentina', the ground-up roots of which make orris, a fixative in pot-pourri, and in the *Artemisia absinthium*, once used to flavour the liqueur absinthe. In the days when we rode a lot, we had enough rue to put sprigs into our horses' and ponies' bridles on summer rides to keep flies away from their heads.

❧ ❧ ❧

The taller herbs – fennel, lovage and angelica – have been planted and seeded themselves in the bed behind, where their height is more appropriate. Also in this bed are mandrakes, *Mandragora officinarum* – grown more for the sake of the mythology that surrounds the plant than for any practical use. The aphrodisiac and soporific properties of mandrake juice, Juliet's sleeping potion, were first noted in the first century AD by the Greek physician Dioscorides in *De Materia Medica*. Happily I did not have to resort to using a hungry dog to acquire my plants (anyone hearing the plant's scream as the roots are pulled out 'will surely die before dawn', so the task had to be performed out of human earshot with canine assistance); our original plants came from Nancy Lindsay, who told me to give the roots very good drainage. This was endorsed by Oleg Polunin, who wrote in *Flowers of Europe*: 'They grow in stony places, deserted cultivation.' To emulate this in our Cotswold garden, I dug holes a good spit deep, added coarse sand and planted the roots in this. Each March they reward me, sending up dulgy, or mauve-grey, flowers shaped like upturned bells.

I notice the bees avoid them, keeping their pollen-collecting activity to the generous supply of crocus planted throughout the garden. The dark green mandrake leaves are long (more than 33 centimetres/13 inches) and pointed; when they come through visitors wonder why we have docks in the border! Later still the 'nests' of green tomato-like fruits ripen; they lie with short stalks on the ground, and we wait for seeds to mature. I know I would hesitate to dig my old plants of mandrake with their deep roots; we just collect the seeds each July to sow and produce new plants.

❦ ❦ ❦

We try to keep this border looking full and luxuriant, so it has a background of shrubs in front of the waist-high wall. *Spiraea* × *vanhouttei* flowers in a cascade in April and its leaves turn a spectacular autumn colour; variegated holly gives light at its feet, with ferns beside it and two important variegated-leaved shrubs nearby: *Cornus mas* 'Variegata', now 3.5 metres/12 feet tall, produces an abundant crop of red berries each year. So far we have not tried to clip it back, but one day I may have to. The golden variegated elder, *Sambucus nigra* 'Aureomarginata', we cut to 30 centimetres/ 12 inches from ground level each winter and by summer the new growth is half the height of the cornus. *Symphytum* × *uplandicum* 'Variegatum' is an important feature, too, with strong cream-margined leaves that light up a patch of the border. Like all the comfreys, this form is also a spreader.

Here, after Christmas, the bulbs begin to come through, accompanied by cowslips, forget-me-nots and hellebores. This is south-facing, so the bulbs tend to flower well. We keep to white, yellow and blue. The daffodils remain in and are allowed to increase from year to year. Each autumn we plant tulips, such as the vivid canary-yellow *Tulipa* 'Makassar', which flowers in early May, with Viridiflora 'Spring Green' tulips, ivory-white feathered with green, in front of them. We plant the Triumph tulips 'Yellow Present' near the front so they can be seen closely, and their canary-yellow insides and paler creamy-yellow outsides noticed. We have been especially pleased with *T. saxatilis* 'Lilac Wonder', a low-growing small tulip with a delicate purple and yellow colouring. Other candidates for this colour scheme are the multi-flowered *T. biflora*, which is yellow and white, next to violet and yellow *T. humilis*.

The edging that tumbles over the low wall by the steps includes *Buglossoides purpurocaerulea*, lithospermum, vincas, *Parahebe lyallii*, *Convolvulus cneorum* and *Campanula portenschlagiana* (syn. *C. muralis*). Along the narrow path between this border and the herbs I allow an irregular edge. There are the old peonies, *P. officinalis*, allowed to flop over, and *Helleborus orientalis*, lamium, more vincas and campanulas and *Veronica gentianoides*. A feature where variegated honeysuckle has been allowed to clamber through a clipped *Lonicera nitida* 'Baggesen's Gold' is accidentally enhanced by a bronze fennel growing through them. Two other shrubs, both evergreen, are *Choisya ternata*, which flowers abundantly twice a year, and *Jasminum humile* 'Revolutum' with hardy geraniums beneath. I am especially delighted with the choisya during its autumn blooming, when it is covered with scented snow-white clusters of flowers that show up well against the shining evergreen leaves – crush these to discover their personal fragrance. Between them, two climbing roses scent and make a great display in late June and July. The 'Wickwar' rose opens first; this is a rambler, so needs careful pruning and tying in in winter. By October it will have a wealth of orange berries. The other climber is the robust musk, *Rosa longicuspis*, flowering in mid-July and scenting the air.

❦ ❦ ❦

When Gertrude Jekyll wrote that a garden should curtsey to the house I think she meant that it should be in harmony, in keeping, with the style of the house, but should not outshine it in any way. Our lawn with its four flanking beds I hope does just this. Writing about the garden in *Country Life* in 1967, Arthur Hellyer called these the 'parterre beds', and since then I have thought about them as such. Each of their shapes is almost identical, and each fulfils my criterion of putting on a continuous display through all the seasons, but that is where their similarity ends. Each of the beds has its own distinct planting character and colour scheme, linked by the thread of my thoughts which runs through them all.

The first border (Bed No. 1), by the door into the antiques shop, is kept to medium height so you can see over it and beyond. In spring the flower colours are white and yellow, with the occasional surprise of blue or purple from the bulbs. Large white Dutch and species crocus open on sunny days from January onwards and there are always a few polyanthus and pansies to cheer us on. The evergreens running through this bed are *Euphorbia amygdaloides* var. *robbiae*, *Helleborus foetidus*, the variegated snowberry, which is kept to 60 centimetres/2 feet or so, a santolina surrounded by *Lamium galeobdolon*.

There are early narcissus, cowslips which come later and then, to break the white and yellow theme, two of my favourites bloom together. They are the gold lace polyanthus and *Tulipa* 'Prinses Irene'. The ground is kept covered all the time, and as the bulb leaves fade wonderful hardy geraniums, *G. sanguineum* and *G. endressii*, re-appear among the evergreen *Euphorbia amygdaloides* var. *robbiae* and tradescantias. The geraniums are those 'easy plants' that Nancy Lindsay recommended me to grow. Besides being easy, they are also such good value, flowering all through spring and summer; then in autumn their leaves turn a dazzling bronzy red. Other plants I have added for summer flowering are *Aconitum* 'Ivorine' and *Phlomis russeliana*. They are backed up by the perennial *Anthemis tinctoria* 'E.C. Buxton' – a wonderful addition, for it flowers freely right through summer and, kept deadheaded, will go on until the October/November frosts. *Alchemilla mollis* defines the edging along the house side of this border and is allowed to spill over the paving. Although it has a certain freedom early in the summer, in July it is firmly controlled – cut to the ground before it can cast

The heart of the garden, bisected by the yew walk, consists of four parterre beds, with varying planting and colour schemes.

its seeds in abandon between each crack in the paving or farther into the bed.

Where bulbs have finished, forget-me-nots are pulled out and cowslips dug and lined out in a shady corner in the potager. Then is the moment we add *Penstemon* 'White Bedder' and white cosmos to fill every gap. By this time and even earlier, love-in-the-mist will be starting its six-month display, first with powder-blue flowers, then with round, straw-coloured seed heads and always causing comments. They are hardy annuals, and seedlings grown from fresh seed sown in August will be robust enough to prick out into drifts, together with the tulip bulbs, in late autumn.

❧ ❧ ❧

In the next border, Bed No. 2, the bulb colours in spring are kept to white, cream and pink, with the occasional outburst of dark purple *Iris reticulata* – planted strategically at the corners, so we remember not to disturb them too much when other plants replace them for summer. Their replacements in one corner are diascias, in another *Echeveria* 'Imbricata' mixed between bronze ajuga and white *Epilobium glabellum*. For interest from January to March there are the usual crocuses and several *Helleborus orientalis* chosen for good colour, including an unusual primrose-yellow one. Their evergreen leaves contrast with the narrow spiky leaves of the yellow asphodel. The tulips we choose for here are 'White Triumphator' and the salmon-rose 'Apricot Beauty'.

The straight 'leg' of this border and the one next to it is important as it acts as the division between this 'heart of the garden' area and the wider lawn and wilderness. I did not want the garden to have strictly structured rooms separated by too many wall-like clipped hedges, but I realized the importance in a garden this size of having areas with different themes or distinct characters. To achieve this there had to be divisions, and in both this border and Bed No. 3 these are created informally by a planting of tall flowering shrubs, both deciduous and evergreen.

In this border the evergreens are a 90-centimetre/3-foot dome-shaped phillyrea, a ceanothus, an unclipped variegated holly, a purple-leaved berberis, a tall and wonderfully fragrant osmanthus, and a still small *Sarcococca hookeriana*. The deciduous shrubs are *Lavatera* 'Barnsley', philadelphus and cotinus. As well as giving the 'heart of the garden' an enclosed atmosphere, these shrubs help to create shelter from our prevailing west wind.

᪥ ᪥ ᪥

The next border (Bed No. 3) always has a generous carpet of white Dutch crocus which come up in February through the tulip and the narcissus shoots. The tulips we keep to deep pink lily-flowered 'Mariette' and 'China Pink'. These look well with a dwarf *Prunus* that suckers through the border and blend with the young leaves of the *Berberis* × *ottawensis purpurea*, which marks the south corner. This berberis has two climbers through it, the white everlasting sweet pea and a late-flowering white clematis.

Forget-me-nots also run through the border. The central line of shrubs – again acting as a division – were all planted in the early 1960s, and had we not kept them well pruned they would now be too tall and old-looking. There is a group of golden privet, the common *Deutzia scabra* and *Cytisus battandieri*. Between and in front of these are August/September-blooming monkshood and *Aster novae-angliae* 'Andenken an Alma Pötschke'. There are penstemons and *Lobelia* 'Pink Flamingo', all dug up in autumn, when many cuttings are taken to grow on for next summer's display. Their place is taken by the forget-me-nots and tulips.

This is all in the 'leg' of the border; the shaped area we try to make look very relaxed and informal. As the theme of this area is intended to be a very natural planting, with everything blending in and almost competing with each other, I have used those plants here which will spread and naturalize and require the same conditions. Perhaps I should call it a controlled meadow garden. I get much pleasure from it. Plants like the lovely evening primrose, *Oenothera biennis*, are allowed to put themselves where they wish to, seeding one year and flowering the next. The beautiful but invasive *Campanula glomerata* competes with *Achillea ptarmica* 'The Pearl' and *Acanthus spinosus* – all strong growers that need controlling. For late interest the tall *Chrysanthemum uliginosum* (now *Leucanthemella serotina*) acts as a background for a wonderful blue *Aster amellus* and *Cornus alba* 'Sibirica'. Sometimes I wish that plant names did not change, but in this case both epithets give us information: '*uliginosum*' tells us that this plant likes a moist situation, '*serotina*' that it is late-flowering. Hebes are among the most useful border shrubs, and here *Hebe rakaiensis* creates a rounded full stop on the narrow end. We drop in the intense blue *Salvia patens* as well as *Penstemon* 'Garnet' wherever there is a gap. The joy and benefit of having a small nursery is that there are always plants available to use generously.

This border, although important as one of the parterre beds, has also, on its straight side, become part of the vista from the temple to the fountain. Here again is an instance of a garden division which separates different areas without too rigorously dividing them into 'rooms'. Although the garden curtseys to the house, it must have its own character, its vistas and patterns and open spaces, its ability to flow from one area to another. I want everyone to enjoy the spaces of their garden – never to feel confined by high hedges and too rigorous a discipline.

᪥ ᪥ ᪥

Bed No. 4 – I used to see this from the desk where I worked in the mornings – always gave me inspiration. It is the last to be cut down and tidied, but this has to be done before Christmas as bulbs must be put in. Then the evergreens take on a greater importance. Basically this border was structured round our *Juniperus* × *media* 'Pfitzeriana', the *Acanthus spinosus*, variegated rhamnus, the old perry pear tree and a large group of dark red *Paeonia delavayi*. We put in evergreen shrubs along one side to make the pond garden more secret. Originally planted in 1962, there was a *Berberis gagnepainii* var. *lanceifolia, Chamaecyparis lawsoniana* 'Elegantissima', *Pyracantha rogersiana* 'Flava', *Spiraea* 'Arguta' and another evergreen berberis which was given to me without a name.

Then honey fungus struck, and now this whole scene has greatly changed. First the tree peonies succumbed, then the *Berberis gagnepainii* var. *lanceifolia* (in spring the scent of its flowers was wonderful and the bees descended on it). Then, worst of all, the old pear tree went. I loved this tree for its covering of white blossom in spring, the shade it gave on hot summer days and its tall, shapely silhouette in winter. It was a special feature and I believe it to have been a hundred years old or more. Sometimes if a plant dies or a tree is blown over you may realize the situation is better without it, but I will always miss the pear tree that I knew for fifty years!

Finally the berberis-without-a-name has been attacked by the honey fungus, and when gone it will leave a huge gap. But, true to experience, I believe that corner may look better without it. The two variegated rhamnus have grown up, so will take over the role of concealing part of the view into the pool garden. The blue fence will be more visible and we can use it as a support for *Clematis* × *durandii* and the autumn-flowering *C. tangutica* or the delicate *C.* 'Etoile Rose'. It will be a prime position where every detail can be observed.

In spring this border is less disciplined in colour than the other three. There are always lots of Dutch crocus and forget-me-nots and a mixture of narcissus. The tulips include the fringed 'Burgundy Lace', a rich wine-red with a crystal fringe, 'Queen of Night', a rather dark – almost black – maroon, and the later-flowering 'Angélique', pale pink and white. I pray that the rain will not spoil their charm and that the emerging red shoots of *Euphorbia griffithii* 'Fireglow' will not clash too much with 'Angélique'.

Then, by late spring, the flowers – often overlooked – of the lamiums will be at their best, the leaves of *Stachys byzantina* will have recovered from winter cold, and the yellow Dutch iris and mauve aquilegias round the santolina will be fresh and beautiful. From then on through summer I love the *Papaver orientale* coming through the *Geranium pratense*, and then the delphiniums given to me several years ago by Blackmore and Langdon spire above the leaves of the acanthus, the *Campanula lactiflora* and a variety of monarda that will flower through August and September.

Always I am conscious of the different effects we must try to create, remembering all the time that flowers follow the seasons, usually but not always in the same pattern. Tall yellow daisies, *Buddleja davidii* 'Dartmoor' and a clump of *Persicaria bistorta* (in my early days bought as polygonum) fill the gaps and take care of the remaining spaces. At the end of summer the seeds on the money plant – honesty, *Lunaria annua* – ripen and it is worth spending time flaking the outer shells to reveal the flat mother-of-pearl coins.

By November the perennials are cut down and the framework of evergreen becomes once again the view from my old window.

❧ ❧ ❧

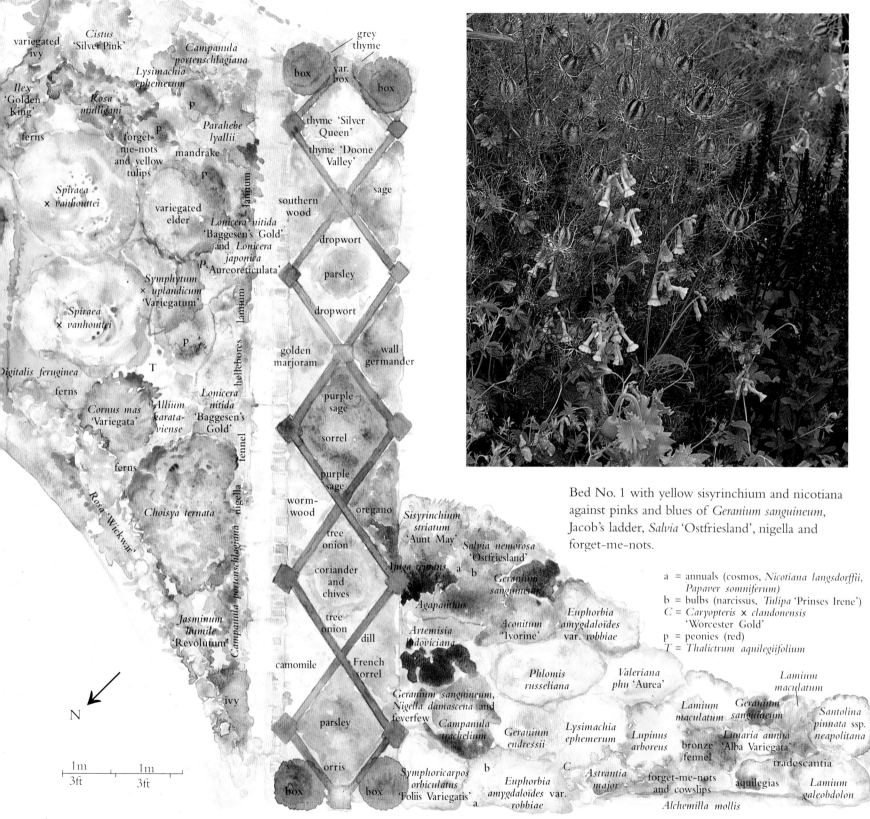

variegated ivy

Cistus 'Silver Pink'

Campanula portenschlagiana

Lysimachia ephemerum

Iley 'Golden King'

Rosa mulligani

ferns

p

forget-me-nots and yellow tulips

mandrake

Parahebe lyallii

p

Spiraea × vanhouttei

variegated elder

Lonicera nitida 'Baggesen's Gold' and *Lonicera japonica* 'Aureoreticulata'

p

Symphytum × uplandicum 'Variegatum'

Spiraea × vanhouttei

p

Digitalis feruginea

ferns

T

Cornus mas 'Variegata'

Allium karataviense

Lonicera nitida 'Baggesen's Gold'

ferns

Rosa 'Wickwar'

Choisya ternata

nigella

fennel

hellebores

lamium

lamium

Campanula portenschlagiana

Jasminum humile 'Revolutum'

ivy

grey thyme

box

var. box

box

thyme 'Silver Queen'

thyme 'Doone Valley'

sage

southern wood

dropwort

parsley

dropwort

golden marjoram

wall germander

purple sage

sorrel

purple sage

worm-wood

oregano

tree onion

coriander and chives

tree onion

dill

camomile

French sorrel

parsley

orris

box

box

Sisyrinchium striatum 'Aunt May'

Salvia nemorosa 'Ostfriesland'

Ajuga reptans

a

b

Geranium sanguineum

Agapanthus

Artemisia ludoviciana

Aconitum 'Ivorine'

Euphorbia amygdaloïdes var. *robbiae*

Geranium sanguineum, Nigella damascena and feverfew

Campanula trachelium

Geranium endressii

Lysimachia ephemerum

Lupinus arboreus

Phlomis russeliana

Valeriana phu 'Aurea'

Symphoricarpos orbiculatus 'Foliis Variegatis'

b

Euphorbia amygdaloïdes var. *robbiae*

a

C

Astrantia major

bronze fennel

forget-me-nots and cowslips

Alchemilla mollis

Lamium maculatum

Lamium maculatum

Geranium sanguineum

Santolina pinnata ssp. *neapolitana*

Lunaria annua 'Alba Variegata'

tradescantia

aquilegias

Lamium galeobdolon

Bed No. 1 with yellow sisyrinchium and nicotiana against pinks and blues of *Geranium sanguineum*, Jacob's ladder, *Salvia* 'Ostfriesland', nigella and forget-me-nots.

a = annuals (cosmos, *Nicotiana langsdorffii, Papaver somniferum*)
b = bulbs (narcissus, *Tulipa* 'Prinses Irene')
C = *Caryopteris × clandonensis* 'Worcester Gold'
p = peonies (red)
T = *Thalictrum aquilegiifolium*

N

1m
3ft

1m
3ft

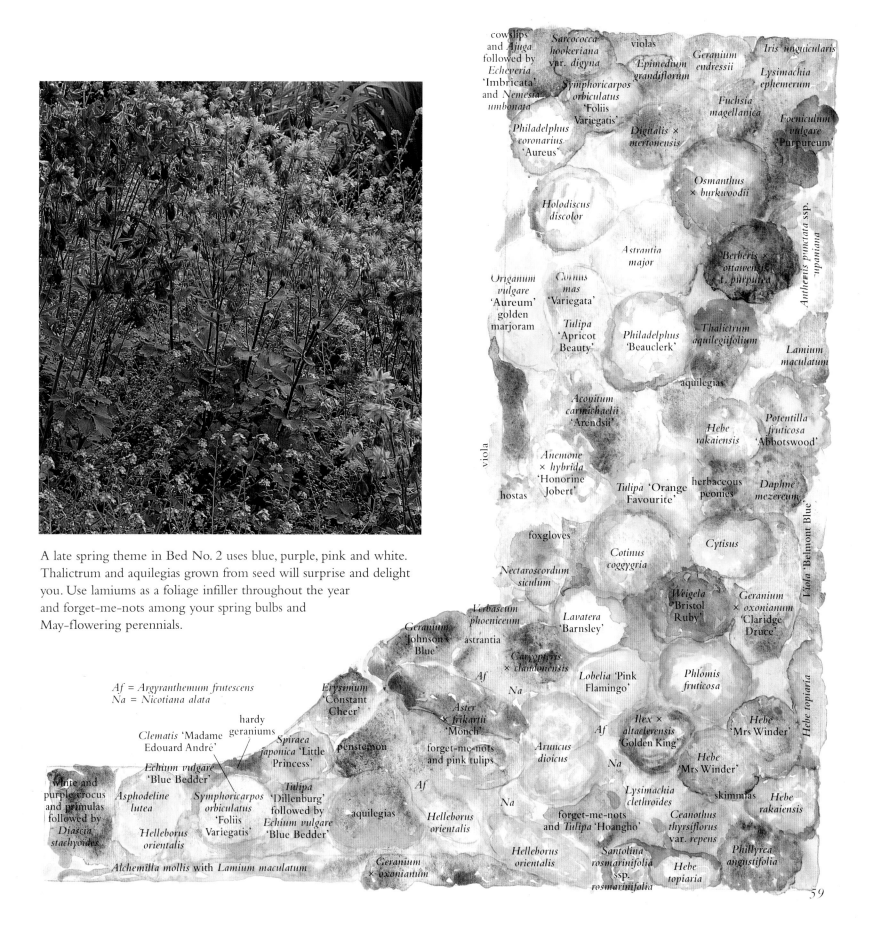

A late spring theme in Bed No. 2 uses blue, purple, pink and white. Thalictrum and aquilegias grown from seed will surprise and delight you. Use lamiums as a foliage infiller throughout the year and forget-me-nots among your spring bulbs and May-flowering perennials.

Af = *Argyranthemum frutescens*
Na = *Nicotiana alata*

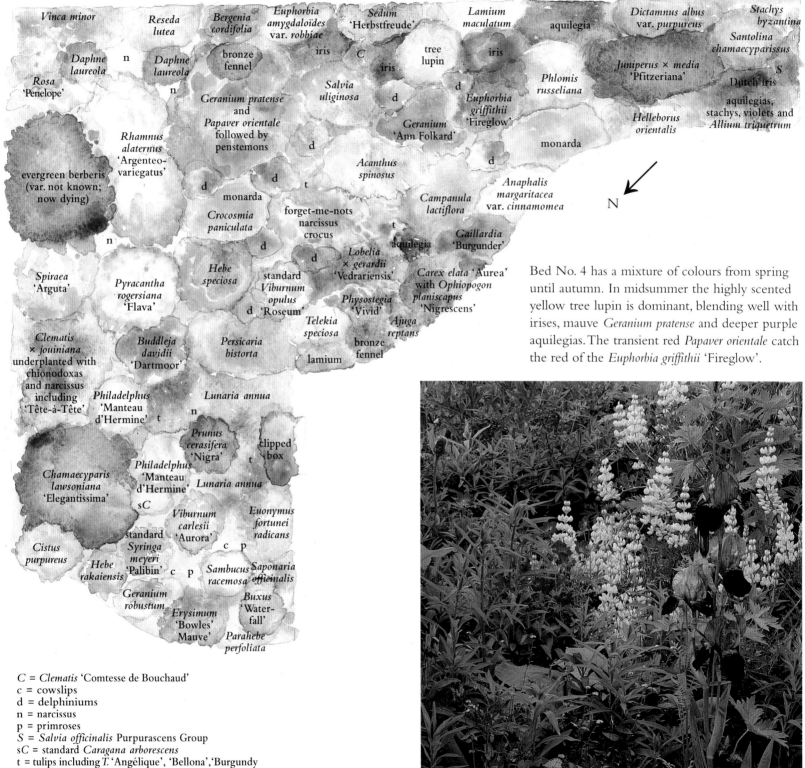

Vinca minor

Reseda lutea

Bergenia cordifolia

Euphorbia amygdaloides var. robbiae

Sedum 'Herbstfreude'

Lamium maculatum

aquilegia

Dictamnus albus var. purpureus

Stachys byzantina

n

Daphne laureola

Daphne laureola

bronze fennel

iris

C

tree lupin

iris

Santolina chamaecyparissus

Rosa 'Penelope'

n

Salvia uliginosa

iris

Phlomis russeliana

Juniperus × media 'Pfitzeriana'

S

Dutch iris

Geranium pratense and Papaver orientale followed by penstemons

d

Euphorbia griffithii 'Fireglow'

aquilegias, stachys, violets and Allium triquetrum

Rhamnus alaternus 'Argenteo-variegatus'

d

Geranium 'Ann Folkard'

Helleborus orientalis

evergreen berberis (var. not known; now dying)

d

monarda

Acanthus spinosus

monarda

d

d

d

t

Anaphalis margaritacea var. cinnamomea

N

Crocosmia paniculata

forget-me-nots narcissus crocus

Campanula lactiflora

n

d

d

aquilegia

t

Spiraea 'Arguta'

Pyracantha rogersiana 'Flava'

Hebe speciosa

standard Viburnum opulus 'Roseum'

Lobelia × gerardii 'Vedrariensis'

Gaillardia 'Burgunder'

Carex elata 'Aurea' with Ophiopogon planiscapus 'Nigrescens'

d

Physostegia 'Vivid'

Clematis × jouiniana underplanted with chionodoxas and narcissus including 'Tête-à-Tête'

Buddleja davidii 'Dartmoor'

Persicaria bistorta

Telekia speciosa

lamium

Ajuga reptans

bronze fennel

Philadelphus 'Manteau d'Hermine'

Lunaria annua

n

t

Prunus cerasifera 'Nigra'

clipped box

Chamaecyparis lawsoniana 'Elegantissima'

Philadelphus 'Manteau d'Hermine'

Lunaria annua

t

sC

Viburnum carlesii 'Aurora'

Euonymus fortunei radicans

Cistus purpureus

standard Syringa meyeri 'Palibin'

c

p

Hebe rakaiensis

c

p

Sambucus racemosa

Saponaria officinalis

Geranium robustum

Buxus 'Water-fall'

Erysimum 'Bowles' Mauve'

Parahebe perfoliata

C = Clematis 'Comtesse de Bouchaud'
c = cowslips
d = delphiniums
n = narcissus
p = primroses
S = Salvia officinalis Purpurascens Group
sC = standard Caragana arborescens
t = tulips including T. 'Angélique', 'Bellona', 'Burgundy Lace', 'Queen of Night'

Bed No. 4 has a mixture of colours from spring until autumn. In midsummer the highly scented yellow tree lupin is dominant, blending well with irises, mauve *Geranium pratense* and deeper purple aquilegias. The transient red *Papaver orientale* catch the red of the *Euphorbia griffithii* 'Fireglow'.

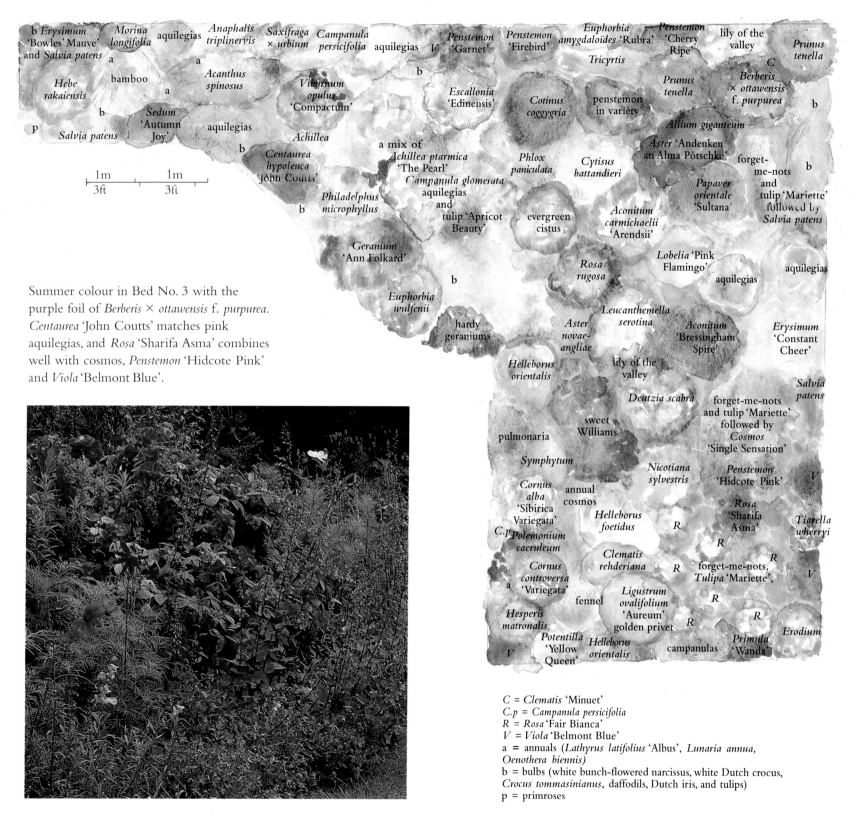

Summer colour in Bed No. 3 with the purple foil of *Berberis* × *ottawensis* f. *purpurea*. *Centaurea* 'John Coutts' matches pink aquilegias, and *Rosa* 'Sharifa Asma' combines well with cosmos, *Penstemon* 'Hidcote Pink' and *Viola* 'Belmont Blue'.

Scale: 1m 3ft 1m 3ft

Plan labels (Bed No. 3):
b *Erysimum* 'Bowles' Mauve' and *Salvia patens* · *Morina longifolia* · aquilegias · *Anaphalis triplinervis* · *Saxifraga* × *urbium* · *Campanula persicifolia* · aquilegias · *V* · *Penstemon* 'Garnet' · *Penstemon* 'Firebird' · *Euphorbia amygdaloïdes* 'Rubra' · *Penstemon* 'Cherry Ripe' · lily of the valley · *Prunus tenella*
Hebe rakaiensis · bamboo · a · a · *Acanthus spinosus* · *Viburnum opulus* 'Compactum' · *Escallonia* 'Edinensis' · *Tricyrtis* · *Cotinus coggygria* · penstemon in variety · *Prunus tenella* · *Berberis* × *ottawensis* f. *purpurea* · C · b
p · *Salvia patens* · *Sedum* 'Autumn Joy' · aquilegias · *Achillea* · a mix of *Achillea ptarmica* 'The Pearl' · *Allium giganteum* · *Aster* 'Andenken an Alma Pötschke' · forget-me-nots and tulip 'Mariette' followed by *Salvia patens* · b
Centaurea hypoleuca 'John Coutts' · *Campanula glomerata* · *Phlox paniculata* · *Cytisus battandieri* · *Papaver orientale* 'Sultana'
Philadelphus microphyllus · aquilegias and tulip 'Apricot Beauty' · evergreen cistus · *Aconitum carmichaelii* 'Arendsii'
Geranium 'Ann Folkard' · *Rosa rugosa* · *Lobelia* 'Pink Flamingo' · aquilegias · aquilegias
Euphorbia wulfenii · b · hardy geraniums · *Aster novae-angliae* · *Leucanthemella serotina* · *Aconitum* 'Bressingham Spire' · *Erysimum* 'Constant Cheer'
Helleborus orientalis · lily of the valley · *Salvia patens*
pulmonaria · sweet Williams · *Deutzia scabra* · forget-me-nots and tulip 'Mariette' followed by *Cosmos* 'Single Sensation'
Symphytum · *Nicotiana sylvestris* · *Penstemon* 'Hidcote Pink' · V
Cornus alba 'Sibirica Variegata' · annual cosmos · *Helleborus foetidus* · *Rosa* 'Sharifa Asma' · *Tiarella wherryi*
C.p · *Polemonium caeruleum* · R · R
Cornus controversa 'Variegata' · *Clematis rehderiana* · R · forget-me-nots, *Tulipa* 'Mariette' · R · V
a · *Ligustrum ovalifolium* 'Aureum' golden privet · fennel
Hesperis matronalis · R · R · *Erodium*
Potentilla 'Yellow Queen' · *Helleborus orientalis* · campanulas · *Primula* 'Wanda'
V

C = *Clematis* 'Minuet'
C.p = *Campanula persicifolia*
R = *Rosa* 'Fair Bianca'
V = *Viola* 'Belmont Blue'
a = annuals (*Lathyrus latifolius* 'Albus', *Lunaria annua*, *Oenothera biennis*)
b = bulbs (white bunch-flowered narcissus, white Dutch crocus, *Crocus tommasinianus*, daffodils, Dutch iris, and tulips)
p = primroses

Scent and food at the kitchen door

Instead of having my herbs scattered around the garden in cottage garden style, I decided twenty years ago to have a bed, formally designed with all the herbs I use most, close at hand and each in its own compartment defined by box. The bed was designed to be directly outside my kitchen; now the door leads into my daughter-in-law's antiques shop. In the foreground (**left**) are different varieties of thyme. The grey-leaved one, brought back from Provence, has a distinctive aroma of its own, especially on hot summer days. The first triangle on the right has *Artemisia abrotanum* and beside it is a good form of golden marjoram. The gold is echoed by the golden leaves of *Buxus sempervirens* 'Aureovariegata'. Sage keeps its attractive form throughout the year, especially the narrow-leaved form, *Salvia lavandulifolia*. In October the wall germander, *Teucrium × lucidrys* is still in flower and the stems of the Egyptian onion have turned straw-coloured. On the right *Choisya ternata* is in full flower, scenting the air as you walk along the narrow path.

Beside the choisya the yellow *Jasminum humile* 'Revolutum' is in full flower in July (**above, left**) and is draped with the extending arms of *Rosa* 'Wickwar' (it came as a seedling from the late Keith Steadman's garden at Wickwar). It is well scented and each flower panicle becomes a spectacular bunch of orange-yellow hips in autumn.

The hollow green stems of the Egyptian or tree onion, *Allium cepa* var. *proliferum* (**above, right**) are topped by clusters of tiny onions – good to add a hint of flavour when chopped and used in your salad bowl. In the foreground are the purple-leaved sage, grey *Artemisia absinthium* and *Origanum laevigatum*, soon to come into flower. Seedlings often creep into the beds, and here *Geranium endressii* has been allowed to spread. We will take care it does not become too assertive.

Flowery meads

The lily-flowered tulips are among my favourites and I try to keep a continuity of colour in each bed so there is an explosion in spring. The pink 'Mariette' tulips (**below**) with their graceful petals flower through the carpet of forget-me-nots (myosotis). This tulip looks wonderful with the opening leaves of *Berberis* × *ottawensis purpurea* and the dwarf almond *Prunus amygdalus* 'Nana'. This

is an area where the tulips are lifted after flowering and the myosotis taken out to leave a wonderful space where we can use some of the annuals we have grown on to make a summer display – cosmos and *Nicotiana sylvestris* – as well as the tender perennials penstemon and lobelia.

Turn round the corner by the berberis, and this bed (**right**), through lack of careful planning, has now become my medieval flowery mead; I know I must not interfere

too much or I will spoil its spontaneity. This lovely pink tulip 'Apricot Beauty' flowers at the end of April with white bunch-flowered narcissus. After the spring bulbs there are *Campanula glomerata* competing with *Achillea* 'The Pearl' for summer flowers, but for early spring we must have plenty of crocus – *C. tommasinianus* are now seeding themselves, and I must continue to add more white Dutch crocus each autumn to make sure that my theory of planting in layers is achieved.

A succession of bulbs

I have been planting more and more bulbs of every sort in the borders ever since our spring visit to Holland in the late 1960s. Seeing the fields of tulips *en masse* with their divergence of colours caused a major turn-around in my thoughts about our garden in springtime. It is hard to resist buying quantities from the autumn catalogues. Each autumn I allow myself a budget – sometimes the emphasis will be on more tulips, at other times on narcissus or the smaller bulbs such as chionodoxas, scillas and the lovely early *Iris reticulata*. However hard we try to keep them correctly labelled, over the years I have lost many of their names, particularly the narcissus, as these are mostly left to multiply in the borders. We find it best to dig up the tulips as soon as the flowers are over and they die down naturally in boxes of soil.

Bed No. 1 (**left**) in mid-April, with the herb border beyond. The colour is always predominantly white through cream and pale yellow to stronger golds here. The narcissus are coming through lamium, aquilegias, *Euphorbia amygdaloïdes* var. *robbiae* and hardy geranium.

The same bed is shown three weeks later (**below, left**). The narcissus are over, their place taken by *Tulipa* 'Prinses Irene' and cowslips. *Lamium galeobdolon* is in flower.

Bed No. 2 (**below**) has a mixture of lily-flowered *Tulipa* 'White Triumphator' and *T.* 'China Pink', with the stronger-coloured *T.* 'Dillenburg' massed in front of a variegated holly and herbaceous plants.

Bed No. 4 (**right** and **below, right**) in two different moods in April. White *Narcissus triandus* 'Thalia' is mixed with the golden yellow daffodil 'Unsurpassable'. *Tulipa* 'Bellona', forget-me-nots and deep mauve honesty surround a standard *Viburnum opulus* 'Roseum'.

Self-seeders and spreaders

We must be grateful to some self-spreaders and beware of others. Two of my favourites, which flower in June, are the perennials *Thalictrum aquilegiifolium* and the scented sweet rocket, *Hesperis matronalis* (**above**). The thalictrum seeds itself, and as the seed heads are attractive we always allow them to develop. Our plants are a deepish pink and I have been promised a white-flowered form, a great addition to any white border. The sweet rocket flowers for several weeks and is especially fragrant in the evening. The RHS *Dictionary of Plants* tells you it is biennial or perennial. We find its clumps increase in size every year but we always propagate more from seed, as an insurance. In the

foreground of this picture are nigella and fennel, both of which will self-sow generously.

Some self-seeders need to be treated with caution. The lovely *Epilobium angustifolium album* (**left**) is dramatic but should be give a place where it can ramp without restraint. Or, if you grow it, as we do, in a border, you must take off the seed pods before they open and proliferate. Look at the flower spike on the left and you will see new flower buds opening at the top while the seed pods are waiting to open. *Acanthus spinosus* is essential in our borders from August through to late autumn. It increases by sending out its fleshy roots all around the parent plant; you must curtail these in autumn or spring or it will take over too much ground.

The alluring white *Allium triquetrum* (**above**) could take over your garden if allowed to seed itself – so don't let it!

Shrubs for structure

These pictures show how important is the use of evergreen and deciduous shrubs in borders near the house. Their shapes create interest and height in winter when the perennials are low, and in summer they make strong background features. They have been used down the centres of Beds Nos 2 and 3 to create a division between the heart of the garden and the larger lawn and long border.

Here (**left**) it is the *Cotinus coggygria* in Bed No. 2 that provides the backdrop. Although I originally planned colour schemes for each of the four parterre beds, inevitably other shades have crept in, and I am amazed at my apparent boldness in allowing them to remain. In this galaxy of colours, the yellow and orange day lilies somehow harmonize with the crimson red penstemon, which together lead on to the paler hazy smoke of the cotinus. This picture is an example of the power of green to bind together colours that are not immediately complementary, compositions at which the Impressionists excelled.

The detail of Bed No. 2 (**right, above**) has the dome-shaped *Phillyrea angustifolia* acting as both a foil and a winter

protection from our prevailing west wind for the May-flowering ceanothus. The blue flowers blend well with the deeper aquilegias. To make these colours vibrate, the pink form of *Thalictrum aquilegiifolium* is left to seed and proliferate freely.

The dominant evergreen in Bed No. 4 (**right, below**) is the Pfitzer juniper, *Juniperus × media* 'Pfitzeriana'. We have removed all its lowest branches to reveal the elegant, more upright ballerina 'legs'. Above, the vigorous growing shoots make a dramatic table top which we must clip back in spring to maintain its important size and shape. Underneath is a mixture of *Helleborus orientalis,* violets, Dutch iris, *Santolina pinnata* ssp. *neapolitana*, aquilegias and *Stachys byzantina.* By July, 1.2-metre/ 4-foot-tall *Campanula latiloba* is surrounded by delphiniums. Fennel is allowed to seed itself in the borders and often makes a dramatic foil for plants with large, bold leaves. Here *Telekia speciosa* has also seeded between the fennel and *Geranium psilostemon.* I would not have planned the bright yellow, rather coarse telekia with these three other colours but it has proved to be a good eye-catcher.

Tall and mound-forming shrubs

The deciduous *Berberis* × *ottawensis* f. *purpurea*, photographed at the end of August, acts as an important pillar at the south corner (**left**); whichever way you are walking past it, you come suddenly on a vista. Other shrubs creating a screen in this bed are *Cytisus battandieri*, *Deutzia scabra* and (not shown) golden privet. This is a place for 'bedding out'– tulips in spring and in summer colourful *Cosmos* 'Sensation' and *Nicotiana sylvestris*.

Sadly, this Bed No. 2 *Populus alba* 'Richardii', its leaves golden yellow above and white beneath (**right, above**) died in 1994. The underplanting is of alliums, yellow tulips, hostas and violas.

Tall shrubs act as a backdrop in the bed beside the herb border (**right, below**). The leaves of *Cornus mas* 'Variegata', margined with creamy white, show off a harvest of red berries in autumn. *Lonicera nitida* 'Baggesen's Gold' (right foreground) reinforces the yellow theme.

Santolina rosmarinifolia ssp. *rosmarinifolia* is in flower in mid-June in the foreground (**below**), and behind the white-flowered, grey-leaved *Hebe topiaria* is evergreen *Ceanothus thyrsiflorus* var. *repens*. All are mound-forming and hardy – this west corner of Bed No. 2 gets the full force of our prevailing wind.

Ground cover

Certain plants are first-class ground cover – they will remain healthy and good-looking from year to year. Apart from dead-heading and keeping the foliage tidy, they will prevent the weeds from growing. Bare soil never remains bare for long, it will always sprout weeds, so why not cover the ground with plants of your choice?

Shown in early May (**above, left**) is *Lamium maculatum* in its purple and white forms, with Alchemilla mollis around it and 60-cm/2-foot *Geranium endressii* behind. All these are easy plants – do not despise them. The alchemilla must be dead-headed to prevent it seeding; we clip it right back in July and new fresh leaves will appear within a few days. Another hardy geranium, *G. sanguineum,* only 35 cm/14 inches high, is good for the front of the border (**above, right**). It flowers for many weeks and then in autumn its deeply cut green leaves turn wonderful shades of red and bronze.

I think of evergreen shrubs with low branches as ground cover. This *Cistus purpureus* (**above, centre**) with soft green leaves is best grown in a poor soil with good drainage; here it is beside a low retaining wall. Its rosy-crimson flowers, with a deep chocolate-coloured blotch at the base of each petal, bloom in a continuous succession through summer and autumn, and harmonise in colour with the blue-mauve *Campanula portenschlagiana* at its feet. This bell-flower has been there for years with no attention except for pulling off the flower stems as they fade.

I like to put ground cover at the corners of the beds (**left**). In spring species crocus push through a carpet of bronze *Ajuga reptans* and then after the last frost, we add the wonderful symmetrically shaped *Echeveria* 'Imbricata'. A small sedum has crept in too.

Another space that cares for itself (**right**) has red campion and white silene mixed with mignonette and self-sown fennel.

Bold colour

All these pictures are of Bed No. 4, where I decided many years ago to put the bright reds and strong yellows together.
In May *Euphorbia griffithii* 'Fireglow' is the eye-catcher (**left, above**) with its bright red flower heads. I am told that it can become invasive, but so far it has behaved well in our border. The foliage adds its contribution to the scene, and when the flowers have faded, the seed heads are attractive too.

The idea of having orange alstroemerias with magenta *Geranium psilostemon* (**left, below**) came from a recommendation in Graham Stuart Thomas's classic book, *Perennial Garden Plants*. The *Acanthus spinosus* is on its way up, and the delphiniums will soon take over.

Oriental poppies are difficult to find the right companions for, but I must grow them for their wonderful buds, their crepe paper-like petals and the way they attract every bumblebee in the garden (**right**). In early morning light in July, the poppies and the yellow tree lupin vibrate together with their bold colours. I wish that the tree lupin, with such a generous flowering, were a longer-lived shrub: at one year old it is good, at two years old it is superb, and at three years old you know you must replace it. Fortunately it grows easily from seed. You can see tall delphiniums and *Geranium psilostemon* through the gloaming. *G. pratense*, on the right, flowers reliably in June.

Autumn treasures

We spend time making our borders look wonderful in high summer: helianthus, heliopsis, asters and other daisy flowers help to keep them alive in autumn, but for the last two years I have been working on subtler ideas to extend our range of plants right through to November. Extending the flowering seasons from summer to autumn to winter is part of my project.

There are salvias, lobelias, *Leucanthemella serotina*, *Lysimachia ephemerum* and several long-flowering annuals. The practical success depends so much on the timing of our first frost, over which we have no control.

The border beside the herb bed in late September shown (**right**) when the *Cornus mas* 'Variegata' was heavy with its cornelian fruits. In front a *Lonicera nitida* 'Baggesen's Gold', kept well trimmed, became a dramatic scene with bronze fennel and golden-netted honeysuckle pushing and climbing through it.

By October (**below**), Bed No. 4, my *laissez-faire* brightly coloured mixture bed, has bold acanthus spikes, tall fennel seed heads and the spiky leaves and flower stems of *Crocosmia paniculata*, a striking plant with small trumpet and orange-red flowers. We are fortunate to have a good form of this.

We must seek out the autumn treasures.

The blue *Lobelia siphilitica* is one that survives our winters and so does *L. × vedrariensis*. Others are not hardy with us, but it is always rewarding to have specimens of *Salvia azurea, coccinea, discolor, guaranitica, involucrata*, in the garden, but mingled with *Aster × frikartii, Caryopteris × clandonensis*, astrantia and the annual *Nicandra physalodes*.

The photograph of Bed No. 3 (**below**), taken on 20th September, shows how much the lobelias can contribute if we are prepared to nurture them. Some hardy (*L. × vedrariensis* and *L. siphilitica*) will self-sow, but others like my prized *L.* 'Pink Flamingo', must be nurtured. We take cuttings in early autumn and these will be large enough to put in the borders after the tulips and forget-me-nots have come out. They will be enhanced by *Cotinus coggygria* behind. Astrantia, *Lychnis* 'Hoar Frost' and *Aster × frikartii* 'Mönch' will still be in bloom, and surprisingly the annual *Nicandra physalodes* we grew at least ten years ago has germinated and is in the centre of this picture in flower and seed head.

The same border (**following pages**), still exciting three weeks later on 14th October, shows a display of the annual *Cosmos* 'Single Sensation' with the tender perennial *Lobelia* 'Pink Flamingo', the hardy 1.2-metre/6-foot tall white *Leucanthemella serotina*. *Deutzia scabra* and the privet *Ligustrum ovalifolium* 'Aureum' are just turning colour.

79

The Temple
and Pool Garden

Our temple has become the most important feature in the garden. It is a quiet place to sit and enjoy the vista to the frog fountain. Discreetly enclosed by the blue railings and gate, it is the focal point when you look back from the fountain along the grass walk between borders and the pleached limes and laburnum. You see this classical building in an ever-changing light, and as the sun moves slowly round you feel enticed towards it. On cloudless days the whitewashed walls are reflected on the pool's sparkling surface.

In its original home, Fairford Park, the temple had no water and the walls were roughcast stone. Built as an eye-catcher two hundred years ago, it was surrounded by trees in a typically eighteenth-century sylvan setting some distance from the house. When we first saw it the stone was crumbling and the central lintel had collapsed, but this did not discourage David from accepting it as a wonderful gift from the Ernest Cook Trust. It arrived here in 1962 on a lorry, each stone carefully numbered. David chose the setting: by good fortune, the proportions of the temple and the geometry of the ground worked perfectly together. The pool, made in 1954, was exactly the same width as the building, and four existing Irish junipers visually helped it to settle into its new surroundings.

When we first erected the temple, I did not fully appreciate how fortunate we were to have it embraced on three sides by our 1770 wall instead of a backdrop of trees. Had I been a trained garden designer I would doubtless have realized the potential of this area at once, but it took me time — some ten years — and the insight of Gay Hellyer, who stayed with us in 1974, to see it in a new light. Gay, with her good eye for space, influenced me to open up the area around the pool rather than cluttering it up with shrubs that

we had room for elsewhere in the garden. Along one side there were four *Buddleja alternifolia* in a row and on the other a veritable forest of *Paeonia delavayi*. Three of the four buddlejas went, and Tim Sherrard exchanged most of the many tree peonies for box balls, which we put along the winter walk.

Now we had more open space, but how to cover the ground? By a happy coincidence, shortly after these changes we visited Gordon Russell's garden at Chipping Camden. The area where we sat for tea was enclosed by hedges and had the same proportions as our pool garden; it was mostly paved, but had pockets left for ground cover and shrubs for shade. Then I read a timely article in the Royal Horticultural Society magazine about laying paving on a bed of dry cement and sand. It was all an invitation to start. Fred and I went off to the farm with my ancient tractor and trailer to pick up a load of well-weathered flat stones and set to work laying these around the pool, just as they are today.

ॐ॰ ॐ॰ ॐ॰

A tree on either side of the temple helps to anchor it — a tall silver birch to the north-west and an ash, *Fraxinus angustifolia* 'Raywood', on the other side. Under the birch is a ground covering of *Buglossoides purpurocaerulea* and some golden privets. In summer we put a seat here so that we can enjoy the scent of the rose 'Camaïeux' that David planted. From Nancy Lindsay came a special large-leaved ivy in bush form which flowers and berries on every branch and has grown into a perfect mound 1.5 metres/ 5 feet high and a little more across.

The one remaining *Buddleja alternifolia* has *Hibiscus syriacus* 'Blue

Bird' beside it with the floriferous *Clematis viticella* 'Purpurea Plena Elegans' making a dramatic show in late summer. The centre hue of the hibiscus flower exactly matches the colour of the clematis. *Magnolia × soulangeana*, planted here in 1962, now has to be kept within bounds. Furry brown flower buds appear before Christmas and eventually open in late April or early May. Over the years they have only twice been spoilt by a late hard frost. Underneath *Campanula rapunculoides* looks delicate between the stones.

Two important trees stand on the south-east side of this garden. The quince swathed in *Hedera helix* 'Goldheart' blossoms well in spring, but sadly we cannot control the disease that makes the leaves go brown in midsummer. The *Gleditsia triacanthos* is one of six I grew from a seed pod I picked up in Madrid's Botanic Garden in 1964. The seeds took well over a year to germinate and I was tempted to throw them away, but at last the warmth and moisture were right and all six seeds germinated within a week. When they were well grown I gave all but one away and we planted this in the pool garden. Now it is a favourite place for one of our thrushes to sit and sing; a true showman, he seems to burst into his best and loudest song when a group of visitors is around.

The paving on this side is more open, but there are still two pockets of *Paeonia delavayi*. Their elegant foliage makes a fresh statement through the summer, and for two weeks in late May the highly fragrant flowers are a talking point. Pick a few, put them on your desk and your concentration will be diverted by their scent. These peonies are always associated in my mind with Hiram Winterbotham, whose eclectic garden at Woodchester, near Stroud in Gloucestershire, was one of the earliest influences of my gardening life. The nine black peony seeds he gave me all germinated. Now we collect our own seeds and sow them in deep trays as soon as they are ripe in autumn. They tend to send down a single strong root first, then a shoot comes up later. In two years they are ready to sell, and in four years they should flower.

The border near the blue railings has several special plants growing in 'layers' to give interest, from *Narcissus* 'February Gold' in spring through to *Rubus* stems in autumn. The 'Dearest' rose is one I grew as a cutting taken from our wedding present to my son

Chris and his wife Jenny. (Its companions were 'Wedding Day', which climbs through a malus in the wilderness, and 'Sweetheart', which is on the garden wall: I thought these a good omen for married life, but quickly took cuttings of all three for myself.) The buttonhole rose 'Cécile Brunner' we also grew from a cutting. Underplanting these are *Allium christophii*, whose huge spherical heads of metallic purple flowers in July develop into prized seed heads for winter arrangements.

The old fig in a corner behind the temple has been there years longer than I have known Barnsley. *Actinidia kolomikta* spreads around the west corner, and a rosemary originally given to me as a cutting from the Garden of Gethsemane seeded itself into the wall above. A yew, also self-seeded, we have clipped into a round shape. Various clematis and honeysuckles survive our cold winters here. *Clematis × jouiniana* takes over the north corner in summer, but in March there are the pink flowers of *Rubus spectabilis*. There are several hellebores and I am always pulling up seedling giant heracleums.

Water seeps through from the pool to the surrounding narrow beds, planted with *Iris sibirica* and *Primula florindae*, with two tall *Phormium tenax* pushing through a mass of bergenia and day lilies.

❧ ❧ ❧

High up on the inner wall of the temple, carved in stone, is the Barker coat of arms, which had decorated the parapet of Fairford Park. David had rescued it before the temple itself arrived here.

Pots and tubs of scented-leaved geraniums and other favourites stand inside the temple. Rupert Golby planted up some terracotta containers for us: two shallow ones have small standard clipped box as central features, one surrounded by wall germander and the other with thymes. Another good combination is a mixture of bronze fennel and Bowles' golden grass.

This is one of my favourite gardens at each time of the day. In the morning I sit in the shade and the sun slants low towards the fountain. Later, as it moves round, it reflects on the pool. By the evening, when the light changes again and the swallows swoop down for a sip of water and the bats accelerate and swerve past you, there is time to pause and feel a sense of peace.

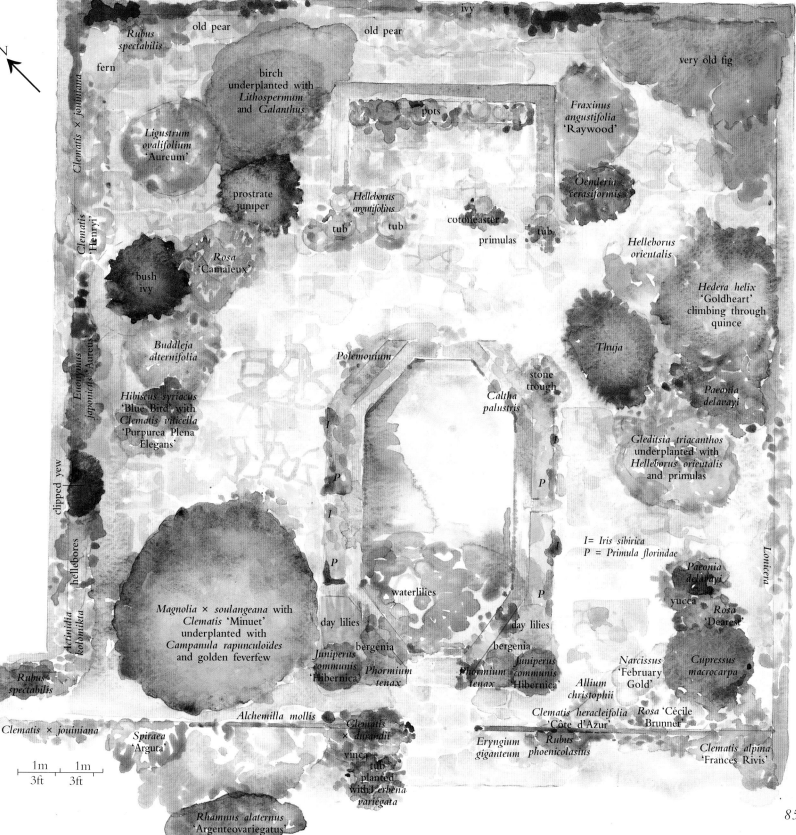

N

ivy

old pear   old pear

Rubus spectabilis

fern

very old fig

birch underplanted with *Lithospermum* and *Galanthus*

Clematis × jouiniana

Ligustrum ovalifolium 'Aureum'

pots

Fraxinus angustifolia 'Raywood'

Oemleria cerasiformis

prostrate juniper

Helleborus argutifolius

cotoneaster

primulas

tub

Clematis 'Henryi'

tub   tub   tub

Helleborus orientalis

bush ivy

Rosa 'Camaïeux'

Hedera helix 'Goldheart' climbing through quince

Buddleja alternifolia

Polemonium

Thuja

Euonymus japonicus 'Aureus'

Caltha palustris

stone trough

Paeonia delavayi

Hibiscus syriacus 'Blue Bird' with *Clematis viticella* 'Purpurea Plena Elegans'

I

Gleditsia triacanthos underplanted with *Helleborus orientalis* and primulas

clipped yew

P

I

P

Magnolia × soulangeana with *Clematis* 'Minuet' underplanted with *Campanula rapunculoïdes* and golden feverfew

P

waterlilies

P

I= *Iris sibirica*
P = *Primula florindae*

Paeonia delavayi

Actinidia kolomikta

hellebores

Lonicera

yucca

Rosa 'Dearest'

day lilies

day lilies

bergenia

bergenia

Narcissus 'February Gold'

Cupressus macrocarpa

Rubus spectabilis

Juniperus communis 'Hibernica'

Phormium tenax

Phormium tenax

Juniperus communis 'Hibernica'

Allium christophii

Alchemilla mollis

Clematis heracleifolia 'Côte d'Azur'

Rosa 'Cécile Brunner'

Clematis × jouiniana

Spiraea 'Arguta'

Clematis × durandii

vinca

tub planted with *Verbena variegata*

Eryngium giganteum

Rubus phoenicolasius

Clematis alpina 'Frances Rivis'

1m   1m
3ft   3ft

Rhamnus alaternus 'Argenteovariegatus'

Pots in the temple

David bought two marble busts to stand in the corners at the back of the temple. Miss Pompeii (**left**) looks across at Augustus Caesar (**right** and **far right**). In winter we use the temple to give protection for slightly tender plants, and colour is provided by primulas in pots. In summer several of our specimen pelargoniums show up well against the whitewashed walls.

In 1993 we used pale mauve as the theme. *Pelargonium* 'Royal Oak' is shown (**left**) and *P.* 'Santa Paula' (**far right**), given us years ago by Joe Elliott, specialist in alpines. The leaves of both are scented.

In 1994 (**right**) we used different reds. By Augustus Caesar's head is *P.* 'Blakesdorf' – a

best-seller for its decorative round leaves. We call the pelargonium on the right-hand side 'A1 Albany', as it came from Peter Coats's apartment in the Albany in Piccadilly. I do not know its correct name, but it has a good leaf. Also here is 'Scarlet Unique' and another unnamed variety with a variegated leaf.

Bronze fennel, Bowles's golden grass and the golden-variegated honeysuckle, *Lonicera japonica*, share a large pot (**below, left**). The same pot is shown earlier in the year (**below, centre**); to its right *Helleborus argutifolius* (syn. *corsicus*), and *Ajuga reptans* have seeded and their roots have a cool run under the paving. *Lonicera nitida* 'Baggesen's Gold' with *Viola* 'Bowles' Black' are in the foreground pot (**below, right**). Above this on the back seat is a foursome pot made specially for us by Whichford Potteries. It is filled with parsley for winter use.

Reflections and water planting

The stone edging around the pond (**below**) has developed a beautiful patina with moss and lichen. Moss covers the edges of the stone trough just visible on the left – it is filled with pink erodiums. The narrow beds around the pool are kept moist by a small amount of water seeping through from the pond. Marsh marigolds, *Caltha palustris*, would take over from the blue *Iris sibirica* if we did not control them.

Looking from the temple across the pond and along the grass vista to the fountain (**right**), reflections in the water repeat the contrast of foliage and shapes. Fastigiate junipers beside the strong strap-like leaves of New Zealand flax are a foil for the arching leaves of day lilies and the round foliage of the water lilies. *Clematis × durandii* climbs through the blue fence, and on the left round heads of *Allium christophii* are a metallic mauve-blue. The *Iris sibirica* around the pool flower at the same time as the *Magnolia × soulangeana*, seen to the right.

Temple views

A long view (**left**) towards the temple with mid-morning light in early June. The pleached lime walk casts an interesting shadow pattern on the lawn. In the foreground of the broad border are *Viola cornuta* Alba Group and a double pale pink Gallica rose, *R.* 'Professeur Emile Perrot'. Farther along the path, the red tinge in the *Acer palmatum* 'Osakazuki' leaves picks up the reddish purple of the berberis.

Morning light and long shadows in April (**right, above**); the sun, still in the south-east, has not yet reached the inside of the temple. Under the *Juniperus* × *media* 'Pfitzeriana' there is a patch of pink lamium and the invasive wild *Allium triquetrum*. Beyond, *Magnolia* × *soulangeana* is in bloom and behind it the silver birch is in young leaf.

I love autumn (**right, below**) with its passing beauty and feeling of peace. The colour change from summer is often dramatic, sometimes short-lived and subtle. Here the leaves of *Acer palmatum* 'Osakazuki' are brilliant for a few brief days, falling to form a crimson carpet. It is so important to pause, absorb and enjoy these moments. The heavy leaves of the limes fall spasmodically. We try to clear them up with the 'Billy Goat' before they blow untidily into the borders, making more work.

The Frog
Fountain and Border

Russell Page said that water in the garden has three functions – reflection, movement and sound. Still water allows for reflection; this we had in the pool mirroring the temple. We had no stream so, to provide movement and sound, we asked Simon Verity to design a fountain at the end of the temple vista with the 1770 boundary wall as a backdrop. A grand feature with water shooting high in the air would not be in keeping with the garden, so Simon devised the idea of water hitting on to a flat stone, which would catch the light and make a gentle splashing sound.

He had in his workyard a piece of spangled Purbeck stone full of fossils, which reminded us of Cotswold sheep's fleeces. This sheep breed developed strong coats as protection against severe winter weather in the Cotswold hills, and their fleeces, traded in Calais, were greatly prized by wool merchants from Italy and France. In the fifteenth and sixteenth centuries, as an expression of gratitude to God for their acquired wealth, the owners of the flocks and wool traders built the wonderful 'wool' churches that are such an outstanding feature of the Cotswolds – such as Fairford, Northleach, Cirencester, Chipping Campden and Burford. Simon made a relief carving of two Cotswold rams from his Purbeck stone, and as a base for this he used dark grey Hornton stone, which looks like lead when it is wet. Judith Verity carved the four fat frogs for the pond sides, ready to spout water on to the rams.

This was the aesthetic part; then the practical work had to be attended to. It was done in record time by three of us – Fred Willis in his early seventies, Arthur Turner in his sixties and me in my fifties. Water could easily by supplied from the swimming pool tap, but for an electricity cable for the pump we had to dig a trench at regulation depth, right across the lawn from the house. Arthur took up the turf but refused to dig the trench, so Fred and I set to. I had no idea whether we would encounter solid rock or soft earth; Arthur suspected the former. However, we were lucky and amazingly there was enough depth of soil to allow us to dig the 45-metre/50-yard stretch in a single morning. This deep soil – so unusual in the Cotswolds – indicated that this area of the garden must have been well cultivated in the past. Fred started digging at the summer house end, I began by the study door, and we met halfway. We laid the cable in the afternoon and then infilled with soil, allowing it to settle for a few days before replacing the turf.

The next major task was to dig the hole for the small fountain pond. Again Fred and I did this, and Arthur wheeled away the soil, which he wanted for his vegetable patch. We lined the pond with concrete blocks and cemented them over, using a waterproof mixture in the final surface. Fred and I, pleased with our efforts, then took a tractor and trailer on to the farm and enjoyed collecting stones to make a natural-looking surround.

❧ ❧ ❧

Simon came on Saturday 4 June 1972, and it was an amazement to us that such a slight, will-o'-the-wisp figure could manoeuvre such heavy stone sculptures. The garden was due to open for the National Gardens Scheme that day. My son Christopher connected up the electricity, and suddenly the frogs spouted. The Cotswold rams had a new wet look. David wrote in his diary that evening: 'Over 300 people came to see the garden, which was looking immaculately tidy and v. beautiful. Everyone was saying how perfect are the colour combinations and layout etc, the laburnum walk almost perfect, and fountain v. entertaining.' Russell Page was right: no garden is complete without the sound and movement that water can provide.

Suddenly the borders on either side of the fountain took on new importance. Before, they were just at the end of the garden; now we and visitors were attracted there by the moving water. The spouting frogs gave a watery look to the area, and although the surrounding soil was no damper than that in the nearby beds, plants had to be added to give an atmosphere of coolness and moisture. I planted lots of *Ligularia dentata* 'Desdemona' and *L. przewalskii* – moisture-lovers that also do well in ordinary border soil. There were already several angelicas and the dramatic giant ferula, and the garden designer Ryan Gainey, visiting me from Atlanta, generously gave me a super specimen of *Aralia elata* 'Variegata'. All these plants have large, important leaves and combine to transform this shady corner into a leafy scene.

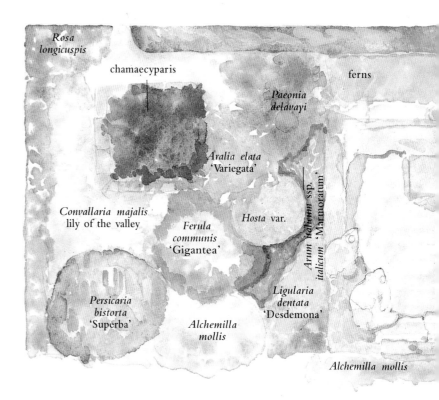

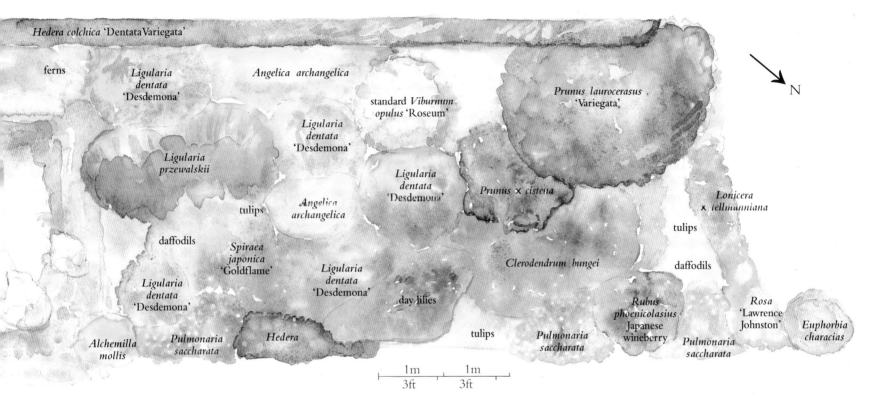

Hedera colchica 'Dentata Variegata'

ferns

Ligularia dentata 'Desdemona'

Angelica archangelica

standard *Viburnum opulus* 'Roseum'

Prunus laurocerasus 'Variegata'

Ligularia dentata 'Desdemona'

Ligularia przewalskii

tulips

Angelica archangelica

Ligularia dentata 'Desdemona'

Prunus × *cistena*

Lonicera × *tellmanniana*

tulips

daffodils

Spiraea japonica 'Goldflame'

Clerodendrum bungei

daffodils

Ligularia dentata 'Desdemona'

Ligularia dentata 'Desdemona'

day lilies

Rubus phoenicolasius Japanese wineberry

Rosa 'Lawrence Johnston'

Euphorbia characias

Alchemilla mollis

Pulmonaria saccharata

Hedera

tulips

Pulmonaria saccharata

Pulmonaria saccharata

N

1m
3ft

1m
3ft

The bright spring leaves of *Spiraea japonica* 'Goldflame' (**far left**) glow among the green and purple foliage of the ligularias, while both prepare to hide the leaves of the spent daffodils.

The frogs, which have been spouting water regularly since 1972, are beginning to have a covering of lichen as well as their moss shawls (**left**). Pulmonaria adds a touch of blue. In April variegated *Arum italicum* ssp. *italicum* 'Marmoratum' sprouts through, and the leaves of the tree peony, *P. delavayi*, hang over the water.

Variegated ivy, *Hedera colchica* 'Dentata Variegata', makes an effective backdrop for the border (**right**) stretching along the wall from the gothick summer house to beyond the fountain. By May *Angelica archangelica* adds a leafy pattern to the ligularias and specks of creamy-white tulips.

The frog vista

The approach to Simon Verity's fountain changes through the seasons, with the Bob Dash bed beyond the pleached limes on your left and the golden end of the broad border on your right. Even in winter (**left, above**) the scene is tinged with gold.

In May (**left, below**), white *Tulipa* 'Mount Tacoma' grows with forget-me-nots, violas and *Senecio* 'Sunshine'. Behind, the angelica grows taller every day. On the right, looking at its best, *Clematis macropetala* is growing through golden privet; the red tulips are *T.* 'Schoonoord' and 'Gordon Cooper'.

By mid-June (**right**) ajuga and violas give softer colour. Foxgloves spire against angelica, their whiteness countered on the right by the astrantias. The focal point, framed by *Alchemilla mollis*, remains the same with the familiar sound of water playing on stone – now with a cooling effect on warm days.

As you walk through a garden, each part should arouse in you a different emotion. When I reach the fountain I like to pause awhile on a seat nearby, at the end of the laburnum walk, and feel peaceful, glimpse the house through the trees and know that I have been entrusted this plot for a few years of its life. The enclosing ivy-covered wall, built by the Rev. Coxwell in 1770, is I believe as important to me as it must have been to him.

The Garden Walks

Like most things in this garden, the three main walks have evolved slowly. Each one has happened for a different reason and at a separate time, and all have different surfaces. The lime and laburnum walk came first, then the grass walk from the blue gates to the fountain, and lastly the winter walk.

I suggest that when visitors go through the blue gates out of the pool garden they should turn left and then immediately right, so they walk down the stone path between the ribbon beds – the start of the middle one of three walks. This was well laid out with flat Cotswold stones set in cement and though it is over fifty years old – and may be more, as it has been here longer than I have – it is still as sound as ever.

The path runs parallel to the 1770 wall; this has a kink in it, and so has the path. I am glad it is like this because this quirk adds character and is also the answer to the question, 'Why a single row of limes on one side and a double row on the other?' – to compensate for the slant in the grass walk.

As you start down the path the two narrow ribbon beds on each side are only 30 centimetres/12 inches apart. Neatly edged with box all round, they are planted with blue muscari and 'Groenland' tulips for spring. In summer, after the tulips are taken out and stored, *Salvia patens* are added, and there are pink *Oenothera speciosa* and bright orange-red eschscholzias which reseed themselves each year. The pink and orange I think clash – I would never wear an orange sash with a pink dress – but I have learned from Christopher Lloyd that a jolt and a surprise are often good in the garden. These ribbon beds are separated by four Irish junipers that stand like sentinels and are now taller than the wall.

Next you pass two weeping cherries, *Prunus × yedoensis* 'Shidare-yoshino' (syn. *P. × y.* 'Perpendens'). We have to keep the branches of these clipped back quite hard so they do not take over the pathway. After seeing a dramatic planting of *Erythronium* 'Pagoda' in a Devon garden in 1972, we planted lots of these under the cherries – they are naturally woodland plants, so love to be shaded in summer – and now every April, just before the leaves of the prunus develop, these delicate yellow dog's-tooth violets with hanging heads give a grand display.

❧ ❧ ❧

Now we will be walking between the double and single lines of pleached limes, nine in each line. They are a constant source of pleasure. We call them 'pleached', but I feel this term must have a certain poetic licence. When we planted them they were not given a framework to be trained on; we simply put strings between each tree and tied the branches horizontally to these, and from the start we pruned off all the shoots that were growing outwards and across the path. It was a very simple operation. They are clipped once in early June and again later in the summer to keep a tidy look. But at the second clip, the vertical top shoots are left. They look spectacular all through the winter as they become redder – hence the name *Tilia platyphyllos* 'Rubra'.

The lime trunks are bare to 1.2 metres/4 feet. When you are walking between the trees you have a feeling of enclosure – you imagine you cannot be seen, but your legs are quite visible. We like to cover every space in the garden, so round the base of these limes collections of species crocus, anemones, saxifrage, hardy cyclamen and lots of rue grow. The trees nearest the wall all have spats or leg-warmers of ivy, which is allowed to climb no higher than 45 centimetres/18 inches. I copied this idea from an avenue in a French château, and now I wish we had done it on both sides – or perhaps that would look too symmetrical.

Beyond the limes, we now come to the laburnum tunnel. When creating it, I was not influenced by the laburnum walk at Bodnant in North Wales. I had not seen it then; if I had, ours might have been wider. The idea came from reading Russell Page's *Education of a Gardener*, published in 1962. To mark our twenty-fifth wedding anniversary in 1964 we planted five trees on either side – the gift of my brother Francis Sandilands and his wife Gill – and gave each laburnum a wisteria to climb through it. We have the wonderful colour effect of yellow and mauve together for three weeks, sometimes more, in late May and early June. We have to be careful to prevent the wisteria from twining too tightly round the laburnum stems, as it would soon throttle and kill them.

The underplanting here is carefully worked out for a succession of interest. For spring there are red tulips 'Apeldoorn' and 'Diplomate'. I think it is essential to have white near red for the two to vibrate, so there are white honesty with a variegated white leaf, white hellebores and *Leucojum aestivum*. These are followed by *Allium aflatunense*, with round flower heads that add more mauve at the same time as the wisteria.

The third event is when the hostas come through. Gardening can be frustrating, and in the hot dry summer of 1976, when the lawns became straw-coloured, all the wonderful hostas I had had from Nancy Lindsay were attacked by botrytis and died. They had matured and multiplied, and to replace them all would have cost a fortune. As I so often realize, gardeners are generous people. Penelope Hobhouse heard of our distress and brought me a carload of young hostas that she had raised at Hadspen. I always remember this kindness and think of Penny when 'her' hostas are up and thriving in July after the allium heads have run to seed.

The laburnum comes and goes, and so do the tulips, alliums and hostas, but David's very individual path is a feature throughout the year. When he was working in Pembrokeshire he filled the boot of his car with interesting stones from the beaches there. Cecil Tomblin who was helping us then made a template and kept him supplied with sufficient cement mixture. David created this unique path under the laburnums, each square different, and each one intricate and beautiful.

The focal point at the end of the laburnum walk is a stone pillar celebrating David's sixtieth birthday, on which Simon Verity has carved John Evelyn's words:

> *As no man can be miserable that is master*
> *of a Garden here; so will no man ever be*
> *happy who is not sure of a Garden hereafter ...*
> *Where the first Adam fell the second rose.*

I have described the most detailed walk – the central one which, were I a visitor, I would choose to walk down at every season of the year to see its changing look, before pausing for a while on the rather damp stone seat at the end, overhung with *Rosa longicuspis*.

❧ ❧ ❧

Now it is time to walk back. In winter and spring, choose the brick path by the wall with narrow beds each side, which we call the winter walk. In January winter aconites will give the first colour, then other early plants emerge – dog's-tooth violets and mandrake, primula and ajuga. The *Ribes laurifolium* is coming into flower, and later many aquilegias and the hellebores – *orientalis*, *argutifolius* and *foetidus* – are looking their best. The pulmonarias vary from white to pink and blue; *Pulmonaria rubra* is often out early enough to enliven my Christmas bunch.

After these beds have been cut down and mulched, a task we aim to achieve by Christmas, the twenty box balls on each side dominate and accentuate the brick path – this is why it is called the winter walk. It came about when on Gay Hellyer's suggestion we opened up and paved the pool garden. This was when we did an exchange with Tim Sherrard's nursery, swopping most of the *Paeonia delavayi* plants dug up from the pool garden for enough five- or six-year-old plants of dwarf box (*Buxus sempervirens*

'Suffruticosa') to clip into balls to line this path.

At the end of the brick path are two stone obelisks carved by Simon Verity. Overhanging them is one of my favourite willows, *Salix daphnoïdes* 'Aglaia'. I took cuttings from Peter Birchall's garden at Cotswold Farm; these flourished and now every February I wait for the pale purple catkins to open and know that on a sunny day flocks of honey bees will come from their home in the south-west gable to gather the pollen. The way from here up to the pool garden is a grass walk – you pass by the stone statues and the blue iron gates and can quietly enjoy the climbers up the wall.

❧ ❧ ❧

The third walk is now the vista from the temple. Percy Cane explained that you should always use the longest possible distance across the garden to full advantage. This influenced us in choosing the site for the temple. We eventually opened up the view across the pool and on to the north-west-facing wall – a distance of almost a hundred yards. This involved removing the lonicera hedge and my mother-in-law's fruit bushes so that we could sit in the temple and contemplate the effect. Eventually Simon Verity made us the frog fountain as a terminal focal point, which also brought the movement and sound of water to our garden.

It all happened in slow stages. The temple came here in 1962. Next the old lonicera hedge surrounding the old fruit and vegetable garden was removed; then in the autumn of 1968 we sowed grass seed to create the long grass walk. For four years a statue of a child borrowed from my daughter Davina served as focal point, but it was too small in scale for the length of the view, so we commissioned Simon to design and make the fountain – ten years after the temple was put in place.

Strolling along this grass path you first see on your right the south-east sides of parterre Beds Nos 3 and 4. As you cross the rock-rose path you have a full view of the façade of the house, framed by the fastigiate yews planted in 1946. To your left are the pleached limes, and then the laburnum walk. But you have two more vistas. First, looking right, you see the grey cedar planted during the war. Walk on, and on your right is the broad border, which is divided by another vista. Here we cut a hole in the hedge to reveal the statue of the hunting lady in the distance. She is on the far side of the lawn and had to be given a substantial plinth to compensate for the fall of the land. Walk on farther, and if you turn right you will be back on the main lawn, with a clear view of the south-west end of the house and its castellated verandah. This is a distinct change of mood, from detailed planting and formality to the open space of the croquet lawn.

If it is afternoon I like to make a U-turn when I reach the fountain so that the sun will be behind me, and then return back along the grass walk towards the temple beyond the blue gates. This way I see each bed from a different angle and will notice more detail in these thickly planted borders.

1 = *The Ribbon Beds*
2 = *The Lime Walk*
3 = *The Winter Walk*
4 = *The Laburnum Walk*

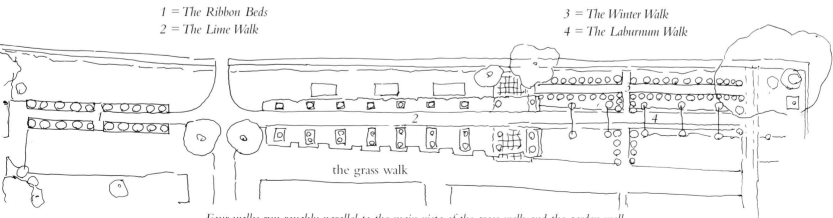

the grass walk

Four walks run roughly parallel to the main vista of the grass walk and the garden wall.

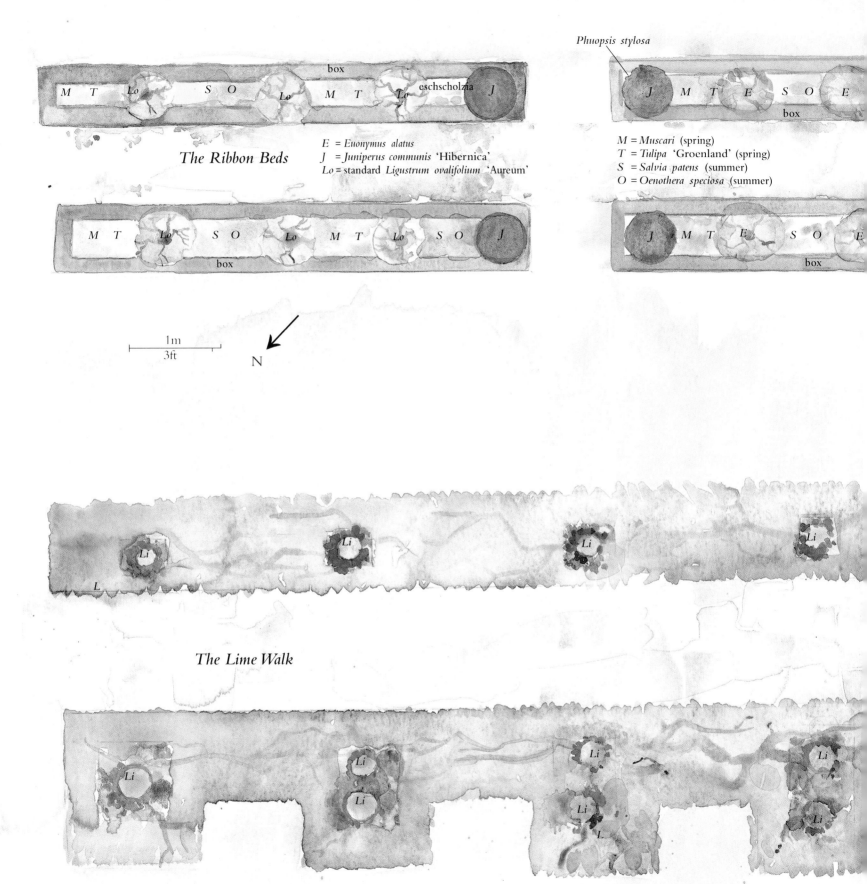

The Ribbon Beds

box

M T Lo *S O* Lo *M T* Lo eschscholzia *J*

box

M T Lo *S O* Lo *M T* Lo *S O* *J*

E = *Euonymus alatus*
J = *Juniperus communis* 'Hibernica'
Lo = standard *Ligustrum ovalifolium* 'Aureum'

Phuopsis stylosa

J *M T E* *S O* *E*

box

M = *Muscari* (spring)
T = *Tulipa* 'Groenland' (spring)
S = *Salvia patens* (summer)
O = *Oenothera speciosa* (summer)

J *M T E* *S O* *E*

box

1m
3ft

N

The Lime Walk

Li *Li* *Li* *Li*

L

Li *Li* *Li* *Li*

Li *Li* *Li* *Li*

L

E S O box pyramid

E S O box pyramid

Prunus × yedoensis
'Shidare-yoshino'
underplanted with
Erythronium 'Pagoda'

Prunus × yedoensis
'Shidare-yoshino'
underplanted with
Erythronium 'Pagoda'

Li Li Li Li

Li = limes (*Tilia platyphyllos* 'Rubra') variously underplanted with
species crocus, cyclamen, violets, rue, feverfew and London pride;
green ivy at base and mown grass between

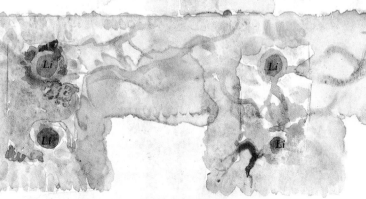

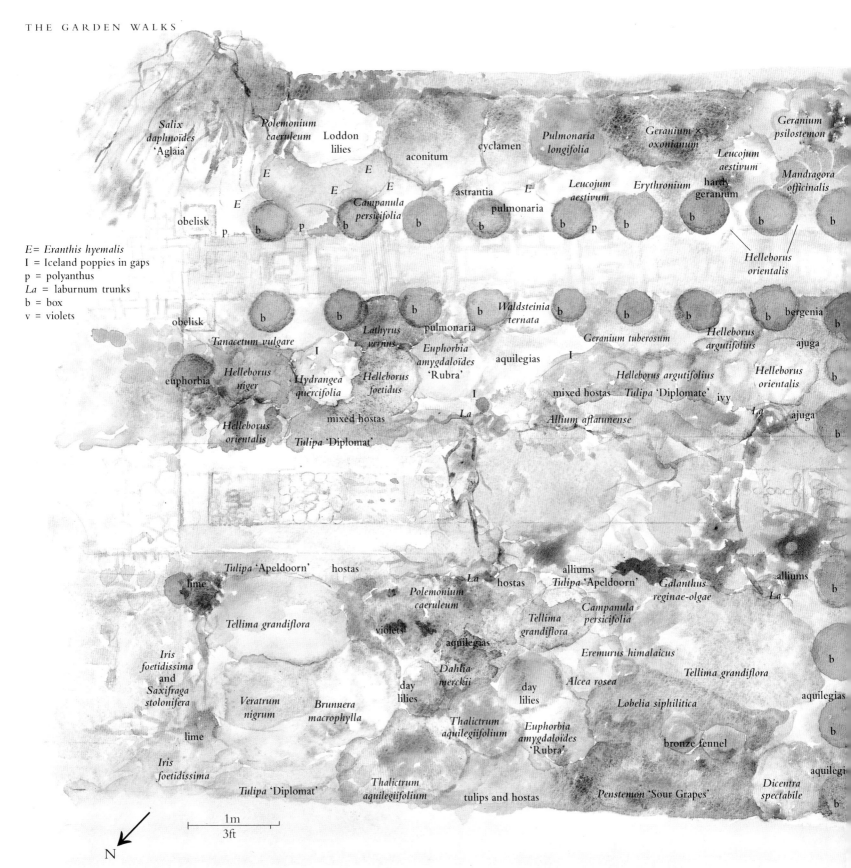

Salix daphnoïdes 'Aglaia'

Polemonium caeruleum

Loddon lilies

cyclamen

aconitum

Pulmonaria longifolia

Geranium × oxonianum

Geranium psilostemon

E

E

E

E

astrantia

E

pulmonaria

Leucojum aestivum

Erythronium

Leucojum aestivum

hardy geranium

Mandragora officinalis

obelisk

p

E

b

p

Campanula persicifolia

b

b

b

p

b

b

b

b

Helleborus orientalis

E= *Eranthis hyemalis*
I = Iceland poppies in gaps
p = polyanthus
La = laburnum trunks
b = box
v = violets

obelisk

b

b

b

b

Waldsteinia ternata

b

b

b

bergenia

Tanacetum vulgare

Lathyrus vernus

pulmonaria

Geranium tuberosum

Helleborus argutifolius

ajuga

I

Euphorbia amygdaloïdes 'Rubra'

aquilegias

I

Helleborus argutifolius

Helleborus orientalis

euphorbia

Helleborus niger

Hydrangea quercifolia

Helleborus foetidus

I

mixed hostas

Tulipa 'Diplomate'

ivy

b

Helleborus orientalis

mixed hostas

La

Allium aflatunense

La

ajuga

Tulipa 'Diplomat'

b

Tulipa 'Apeldoorn'

hostas

La

hostas

alliums

Tulipa 'Apeldoorn'

Galanthus reginae-olgae

alliums

La

b

lime

Polemonium caeruleum

Tellima grandiflora

Campanula persicifolia

Tellima grandiflora

violets

aquilegias

Eremurus himalaicus

Tellima grandiflora

b

Iris foetidissima and *Saxifraga stolonifera*

Dahlia merckii

day lilies

day lilies

Alcea rosea

Lobelia siphilitica

aquilegias

Veratrum nigrum

Brunnera macrophylla

Thalictrum aquilegiifolium

Euphorbia amygdaloïdes 'Rubra'

b

lime

bronze fennel

Iris foetidissima

aquilegi

Tulipa 'Diplomat'

Thalictrum aquilegiifolium

tulips and hostas

Penstemon 'Sour Grapes'

Dicentra spectabile

b

1m
3ft

N

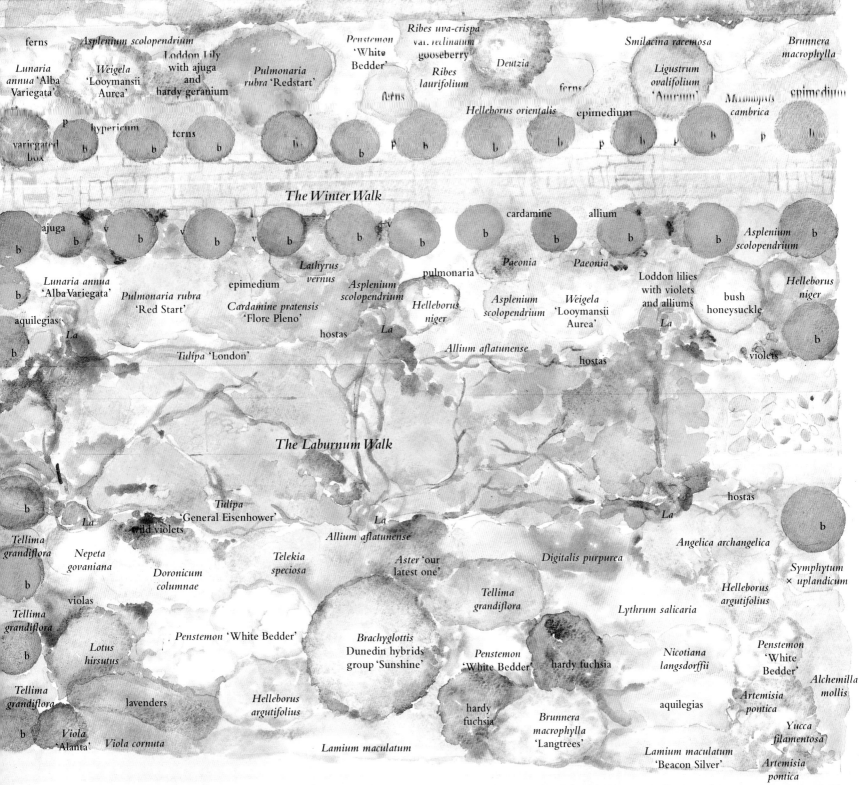

ferns

Asplenium scolopendrium

Loddon Lily
with ajuga
and
hardy geranium

Penstemon
'White
Bedder'

Ribes uva-crispa
var. reclinatum
gooseberry

Smilacina racemosa

Brunnera
macrophylla

Lunaria
annua 'Alba
Variegata'

Weigela
'Looymansii
Aurea'

Pulmonaria
rubra 'Redstart'

Deutzia

Ribes
laurifolium

Ligustrum
ovalifolium
'Aureum'

Meconopsis
cambrica

epimedium

ferns

Helleborus orientalis

epimedium

p

hypericum

ferns

variegated
box

p   b   b   b   b   b   b   h   b   b   b   b   p   h   b   p   b   p   h

The Winter Walk

ajuga   b   v   b   v   b   v   b   b   cardamine   b   allium   b   v   b   Asplenium   b
scolopendrium

b   Lunaria annua
'Alba Variegata'

Pulmonaria rubra
'Red Start'

epimedium

Lathyrus
vernus

Asplenium
scolopendrium

pulmonaria

Paeonia   Paeonia

Loddon lilies
with violets
and alliums

Helleborus
niger

aquilegias   Cardamine pratensis
'Flore Pleno'

Helleborus
niger

Asplenium
scolopendrium

Weigela
'Looymansii
Aurea'

bush
honeysuckle

La   La

b   hostas   La   La

b   Tulipa 'London'

Allium aflatunense   hostas   violets   b

The Laburnum Walk

b   Tulipa
'General Eisenhower'   La

Allium aflatunense

La   hostas

b

Tellima
grandiflora   La   wild violets

Nepeta
govaniana

Telekia
speciosa

Aster 'our
latest one'

Digitalis purpurea

Angelica archangelica

Symphytum
× uplandicum

b   Doronicum
columnae

violas

Tellima
grandiflora

Tellima
grandiflora

b   Lotus
hirsutus

Penstemon 'White Bedder'

Brachyglottis
Dunedin hybrids
group 'Sunshine'

Tellima
grandiflora

Penstemon
'White Bedder'   hardy fuchsia

Lythrum salicaria

Helleborus
arguitfolius

Nicotiana
langsdorffii

Penstemon
'White
Bedder'

Alchemilla
mollis

b   lavenders

Helleborus
arguitfolius

hardy
fuchsia

Brunnera
macrophylla
'Langtrees'

aquilegias

Artemisia
pontica

b   Viola
'Alanta'   Viola cornuta

Lamium maculatum

Lamium maculatum
'Beacon Silver'

Yucca
filamentosa

Artemisia
pontica

The 'Bob Dash' Bed

Seasonal walks

Winter is a quiet time in the garden except for those who enjoy the earliest flowers and an appreciation of the structures. In March the winter walk comes alive with *Leucojum aestivum*, *Helleborus argutifolius* and *H. orientalis* and *Pulmonaria* 'Sissinghurst', backing up the low avenue of balls of clipped box, *Buxus sempervirens* 'Suffruticosa' (**left, below**).

By April nature moves on (**right**). The borders on each side of the grass walk from the fountain to the temple are becoming full of colour. *Clematis alpina* covers the clipped golden privet and .beyond this *Lonicera nitida* 'Baggesen's Gold' stands out in front of *Tulipa* 'Gordon Cooper'. These echo the red tulips under the laburnum and your eye is taken towards the temple. On the right, the Bob Dash bed has forget-me-nots and the double white tulip 'Mount Tacoma' and ajugas coming into flower.

By autumn, when the evening sun is low (**left, above**), I enjoy the statues, the tall Irish junipers contrasting in shape with the weeping cherries. In the background the leaves of the silver birch have already turned a soft gold. *Geranium procurrens*, still flowering on the wall on the right, blends with the golden ivy and *Clematis* 'Jackmanii' growing over the iron gate.

Along the lime and laburnum walks

Looking along the winter walk on a winter's day before human footprints have spoilt the light snow covering (**left**), you can almost hear the silence. Snow rests on every branch and twig of the limes in the foreground and on the birch, the ash and the chamaecyparis in the background, silhouetted against the clear blue sky.

Early morning sun at the beginning of the year lights up the startling red twigs on the limes (**far left**). The bases of their trunks are embraced by spats of ivy clipped to 40 cm/ 16 inches high, and around them are species crocus that come through each February. In the foreground the stone pillar is one of a pair carved by Simon Verity

Now, in late May (**below**), the lime trees are in full leaf. The round *Allium aflatunense* heads stand tall over the finely cut leaves of tanacy, *Tanacetum vulgare*, dark aquilegias and euphorbia. Some of the limes on the farther side have *Lonicera nitida* clipped into squares.

In each season the laburnum tunnel (**following pages**) has a different mood and emphasis. In winter (**left**) the path made by David with its unique pattern of stones is as important as the tracery of the laburnum branches. In April and early May (**centre**) the bright red tulip 'Apeldoorn' stands out as a surprise – red must have plenty of green to soften it, and white to help it vibrate. In June (**right**) the mood and colour scheme quickly change as the upright *Allium aflatunense* come into flower under the canopy of the hanging laburnum flowers.

The Walls

I constantly appreciate how lucky we are to have our wonderful garden wall, and feel grateful that in 1770 the Rev. Charles Coxwell had the foresight to build this 2.1-metre/7-foot high boundary on three sides of the garden. The cut Cotswold stone of the wall has survived well, the key factor being the beautiful coping stones along the top, laid horizontally and mortared together. Their slight wedge-shape encourages rain to drip off rather than seeping down inside. Our Cotswold stone is porous, and damage will occur whenever damp infiltrates into the smallest crack, freezes, then expands and bursts its confines, as with water pipes. After finding some deterioration at the top of the wall in about 1960, we had the coping stones relaid, and some replaced, and they should now serve their purpose for another century or more.

The main stretch of wall faces north-west, and you might think this less than ideal for growing climbers. I thought so way back in the 1950s, but I was wrong. The sun may not reach this aspect until after midday in summer, but then it is there till sunset.

❀❀ ❀❀ ❀❀

Every new scheme must have some starting point. It may be a culmination of themes gathered from other gardens, or a certain impact from just one garden – which was the case here. One magical evening in the early 1970s, David and I called in at Pyrford Court, a garden where Gertrude Jekyll had once worked. Mr Chick, who had been head gardener for decades, took us round, and here I first became aware of the potential of growing shrubs against a wall. I came home and immediately embarked on filling every possible space on our boundary wall.

You can see from the planting plans the shrubs we have used. Some are genuine climbers, while others are shrubs usually grown as free-standing specimens – though hardy, they come into flower earlier, appreciating the wall protection. Plenty of permanent support is essential for climbers: it is no good having to fetch another nail and piece of string every time a clematis sends out a new long shoot that needs to be tied in. We solved the problem by attaching lengths of old pig wire netting to the wall, using staples to do this. New netting would have been too obvious, but the old pieces had a weathered look that blended unobtrusively into the stone. Now, twenty years on, as Les and I walk along the wall wondering where we can fit in yet another clematis or annual sweet pea, we always have strings or ties in our pockets, and any waving branches are immediately controlled.

❀❀ ❀❀ ❀❀

Everywhere in the garden it is important to look upwards as well as down, and I know equally well that planting under the climbers is vital. At first hefty clumps of *Helleborus orientalis* and *H. argutifolius* (then *H. corsicus*), together with wonderful Barnhaven primroses that came my way at the same time, formed the basic structure of the underplanting. Now they are augmented with London pride, pachyphragma, sisyrinchium and Jacob's ladder – all plants that will thrive in a dry, semi-shady situation.

The non-climbing shrubs we have planted in the narrow bed at the foot of the wall are the American beauty bush, *Kolkwitzia amabilis*, *Buddleja davidii* 'Peace', *Ceanothus* × *delileanus* 'Gloire de Versailles', *Ribes laurifolium*, several deutzias, *Mahonia japonica*, *Itea*

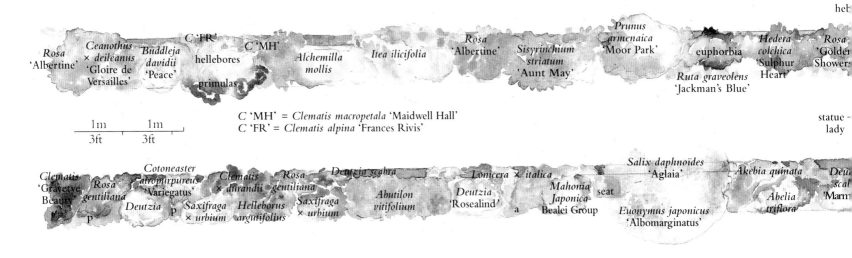

heb

Rosa 'Albertine' · Ceanothus × deileanus 'Gloire de Versailles' · Buddleja davidii 'Peace' · C 'FR' · hellebores · primulas · C 'MH' · Alchemilla mollis · Itea ilicifolia · Rosa 'Albertine' · Sisyrinchium striatum 'Aunt May' · Prunus armenaica 'Moor Park' · euphorbia · Ruta graveolens 'Jackman's Blue' · Hedera colchica 'Sulphur Heart' · Rosa 'Golden Showers'

C 'MH' = *Clematis macropetala* 'Maidwell Hall'
C 'FR' = *Clematis alpina* 'Frances Rivis'

1m / 3ft   1m / 3ft

statue - lady

Clematis 'Gravetye Beauty' · Rosa gentiliana · Cotoneaster atropurpureus 'Variegatus' · Deutzia · p · Clematis × durandii · Saxifraga × urbium · Helleborus argutifolius · Rosa gentiliana · Saxifraga × urbium · Deutzia scabra · Abutilon vitifolium · Deutzia 'Rosealind' · a · Lonicera × italica · Mahonia japonica Bealei Group · seat · Euonymus japonicus 'Albomarginatus' · Salix daphnoïdes 'Aglaia' · Akebia quinata · Abelia triflora · Deu scal 'Marm

ilicifolia and a variegated *Cotoneaster atropurpureus* which is trained up the wall. By the gate leading towards the potager, the perennial *Geranium procurrens* – whose natural habit is to make a rampant ground cover – is successfully encouraged to grow upwards by poking or tying its shoots into the netting; through the summer and autumn it makes more and more growth, nearly to the top of the wall, and is covered with attractive pale purple flowers.

There are days in June and July when the roses on the wall are wonderful, both for their scent and for their display. In the early days I bought a collection of climbers including yellow *Rosa* 'Gloire de Dijon', and the dramatic violet-mauve rambler 'Veilchenblau'. I added the indispensable 'Albertine', a lovely coppery-salmon, and the vigorous creamy-white *R. gentiliana*: both of these are ramblers, and require the same treatment. They must be pruned to match their vigour, with most of the old branches taken out to allow the young growth the chance to spread and bloom.

On the wall, *Rosa* 'Veilchenblau' flowers by the honeysuckle *Lonicera* × *brownii* 'Dropmore Scarlet'. Their two colours – violet and scarlet – together make a disturbing, almost violent, impact in contrast to the grey, blue and pink theme in the rest of the garden. Another good combination is the yellow and purple of *R.* 'Golden Showers' with *Clematis* 'Jackmanii', both pushing their way through

Hedera colchica 'Sulphur Heart'.

David often became inspired to have a certain plant after reading a description by Vita Sackville-West, and on one occasion he came to me saying, "We must have a 'Moor Park' apricot." He had been reading Jane Austen. I gave him one for a birthday present, but had a hard time placing it; first it went by our kitchen door, then, as it outgrew its space, it was planted near the iron gate in this north-west-facing wall. It has excelled itself in vigour but not in fruit production, so I know I must consult Bob Sherman, the fruit expert at Ryton.

Another excitement comes with the early clematis. We have a lovely clear blue *C. macropetala* 'Maidwell Hall' which gives a fine display, and near by is *C. alpina* 'Frances Rivis', a violet-blue with white stamens. Both these clematis, which flower in spring, need very little pruning, but to tidy them, cut back immediately after flowering so that they have time to make new growth for next year.

A wall provides protection and enclosure and can also be a great planting opportunity. But you must be willing to devote ample working time to it, and ensure plant roots have enough moisture – we play a sprinkler on to ours in dry spells. Remember also to allow yourself time to stand and absorb the impact of the flowers and foliage displayed against their solid textural background.

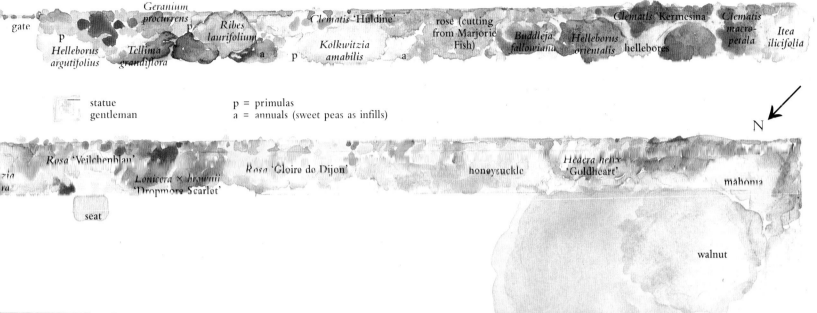

Clematis 'Jackmanii'

gate

p
*Helleborus
argutifolius*

*Tellima
grandiflora*

*Geranium
procurrens*

p

*Ribes
laurifolium*

a

p

*Kolkwitzia
amabilis*

Clematis 'Huldine'

a

rose (cutting
from Marjorie
Fish)

*Buddleja
fallowiana*

*Helleborus
orientalis*

helledores

Clematis 'Kermesina'

*Clematis
macro-
petala*

*Itea
ilicifolia*

☐— statue
gentleman

p = primulas
a = annuals (sweet peas as infills)

N

Rosa 'Veilchenblau'

zia
ia

*Lonicera × brow011
'Dropmore Scarlet'*

Rosa 'Gloire de Dijon'

honeysuckle

*Hedera helix
'Goldheart'*

mahonia

seat

walnut

The long wall border is narrow,
only 40 cm/16 ins, but wide
enough to have low plants at the
feet of all the shrubs that grow
against the wall. This prevents us
from seeing bare stems and
encourages downward as well as
upward glances.

The seedling euphorbia turns
a vibrant shade by October and
contrasts well with the grey *Ruta
graveolens* 'Jackman's Blue' (**far
left**); we cut off the rue flowers
to keep the plants bushy.

Farther along, the foliage of
Helleborus argutifolius (it flowers
from January until spring) covers
the stems of the rambler *Rosa
gentiliana* (**left**). We allow all the
primroses, primulas and the
hellebores to seed themselves,
but the soil must be kept moist
enough in dry summers or they
will disappear. Any seedlings that
appear in the lawn are dug up
and potted on for sale.

Climbers for walls

Honeysuckles, roses and clematis play the chief roles in my wall planting, backed up by buddlejas, kolkwitzia and ivies. *Hedera colchica* 'Sulphur Heart' is extremely vigorous, scrambling up the wall together with *Rosa* 'Golden Showers'(**far left**). Later the *Clematis* 'Perle d'Azur' flowers further along the wall.

A honeysuckle (**left, top**) is in full flower in mid-May. I bought this as *Lonicera × americana*, but after consulting with Tony Lord, who helps us constantly with naming, he tells me it should be *Lonicera × italica*. It has a strong scent which wafts towards you.

The genus clematis must surely contribute as much as any to our gardens. I like to plant more and more each spring. This *Clematis macropetala* 'Maidwell Hall' (**left, centre**) has grown on our wall for twenty years; and I know it will be in flower during Chelsea week in May. Later in the year the fluffy seed heads make a soft display.

There is a surprise and even a shock when mauve *Rosa* 'Veilchenblau', the honeysuckle *Lonicera* 'Dropmore Scarlet' and the puce-coloured hardy *Geranium psilostemon* all flower together (**right**). Photographed here on 15 July, they make a striking trio opposite the laburnum walk.

Itea ilicifolia shown in flower (**above, left**) is a climber I first learnt about at Pyrford Court. Bring some long flowering tassels indoors in autumn and they will scent your room. *Sedum telephium* is the pink-flowered companion at its feet.

Kolkwitzia amabilis, the American beauty bush, is usually grown as a free-standing shrub; we have it like this elsewhere in the garden, but it is also a success trained against our north-west-facing wall (**above, right**).

We encourage the prostrate *Geranium procurrens* (**above, left**) to grow upwards, twining through netting to make a delicate tracery of green and magenta against the lichen covered stone wall. It makes a wonderful impact from June through until late autumn.

This almost white *Deutzia* (**above, right**) I brought home as cuttings from a garden in Herefordshire, where the owner, Mrs Cadbury, specializes in unusual shrubs. This *Deutzia* flowers profusely in June and July growing against our north-west facing wall.

The Broad Border

The broad border was planted in the winter of 1969. This area had been part of the old fruit garden and was enclosed on two sides by a straggly hedge of *Lonicera nitida*. It was quite a problem: you had to fight your way through a forest of ground elder to pick the berries and currants. When we decided to open up the long axis from the temple to where the frog fountain now plays – a major breakthrough in the design of the whole garden – we had to cut through the fruit patch and it seemed time to eradicate the entire feature and rethink the area.

The lonicera hedge came out in 1964 – the year the laburnum tunnel was planted; the strawberry bed was given a new home and the gooseberry and currant bushes went on the bonfire. I began to clean the soil. With no Roundup in those days to do the job for us, we resorted to our tactic of sowing grass seed here and mowing the patch for a few years to help to eradicate the perennial weeds. I kept a strip of the cleanest part of the ground to line out our rooted cuttings and to use as a seed bed. My daughter Davina helped by keeping the ground weed free, growing chrysanthemums, godetias and other annuals that she enjoyed picking.

When we came to plant the border, we used a selection of bought material, but most was grown from cuttings we had rooted ourselves in the mist propagator our invaluable handyman Cecil Tomblin had set up in 1963.

❧ ❧ ❧

My planning of the broad border was strongly influenced by our visit to Pyrford Court (see page 113), where we walked through the Gertrude Jekyll borders and saw their colour effects enhanced by the light of the evening sun. We saw the golden bed, then, turning a corner, came on the blue and green bed and the border full of hot reds with green. This was the moment when I realized how colours react dramatically with one another and also how important architectural plants are with their different shapes – rounded domes, vertical spires and strong horizontals.

These ideas were in my mind as I planned the planting. It was a wonderful open space, 22.8 metres/25 yards long by 7.3 metres/8 yards wide, bordered in front by the mown grass walk and backed by the yew and beech hedge. David castellated the yew some years later. On the other side of the hedge is an 'L'-shaped bed planted with Rugosa roses which helps to create a vista towards the Gothick summer house built at the end of our eighteenth-century stone wall. We grew these roses from hips given to us by Marjorie and John Buxton from their garden at Cole Park, near Malmesbury. We put the hips straight into the ground in the potager, and when the seedlings were large enough we transplanted them here. The scent of their flowers is wonderful, their leaves turn a magnificent autumn colour and their hips are as attractive to us as to the birds.

❧ ❧ ❧

The gothick summer house, built like the wall in 1770 by the Rev. Charles Coxwell, is a full-stop at the end of the stone wall and probably served as a folly, to be seen from the new front gate in what was at the time a landscape-style garden. It faces due north, so only gets a quota of weakening sun on cloudless summer evenings. I like to think that Mrs Coxwell sat quietly here in order to escape from her nine children. Its façade is reminiscent of a church screen, and children ask me whether it is a chapel. No, I tell them, it is the home of a colony of rare Natterer's bats, which are counted every June by the Bat Society. The stone façade of this building is deteriorating after two hundred years' weathering and will certainly require restoring if it is to last as long again.

❧ ❧ ❧

For the broad border, I divided the area into three and planned to create schemes based on green and reds, green and blue, and finally golds. The sections have stepping-stone paths between them and a winding path at the back, near the hedge, helps to make maintenance and weeding easier.

As well as drawing on my impressions of Pyrford Court, I paid special attention to coloured foliage at the Chelsea Flower Show in 1969. Many of my discoveries there helped me to design the broad border, as well as to create other effects in the garden. With my notes and slowly increasing knowledge I put together a plan.

The border was deep so it was important to compose it carefully. To make the proportions more manageable, I decided to have a semicircle of evergreens, related to each colour scheme and forming a three-dimensional pattern, two-thirds of the way back in each section. Four bronze-tinged *Cryptomeria japonica* 'Elegans' formed the semicircle in the 'red' border. We had seen this plant in Cornwall and were determined to have it.

We grew penstemons from seed to make a wonderful impact all through summer. These were the broad-leaved, large-flowered varieties, deep red and often with white throats; since then I have discovered that the narrow-leaved 'Evelyn' and 'Garnet' are more reliable. We struggled with perennial salvias, which must be brought inside for protection each winter. I put a young *Cotinus coggygria* 'Royal Purple' in the front, and ever since have pruned it hard each spring to enjoy its new growth. The cryptomeria, successful for several years, outgrew their space – they did not respond well to hard clipping – and so came out.

Quite soon I abandoned the ambition for a red border, and the planting was dominated by the cotinus, a cistus, an *Acer palmatum* 'Osakazuki' given to me years ago and which I never expected to

survive our alkaline soil, and the evergreen *Osmanthus × burkwoodii* that has fragrant white flowers in April. Under the osmanthus is a ground-cover patch of sweet cicely, *Myrrhis odorata*. We cut this to the ground in late June, and it immediately sprouts again and makes a second fresh filigree.

For spring there are primulas and bulbs which vary each year. We try to make this corner interesting in summer with more unusual plants – *Morina longifolia*, *Francoa ramosa*, and the succulent *Echeveria* 'Imbricata', whose grey leaves go well with blue *Salvia patens* and white parahebes. For background in 1994 we used a group of *Hebe* 'Amy', with lovely deep claret foliage. This is not hardy, so must be brought in before frost. Behind these the ground is covered with *Trachelospermum jasminoïdes*, *Anemone × hybrida*, aquilegias, foxgloves, the oak-leaved hydrangea and the non-stop-flowering *Veronica peduncularis* 'Georgia Blue', a treasure given me by Dan Hinkley of Heronswood Nursery near Seattle.

I like to feel the garden has many associations – with people who have given me plants, and with places where I have seen exciting planting. The two lilacs in the border are cuttings from the bushes I gave my son Chris and his wife Jenny as part of their wedding present. The *Viburnum henryi* reminds me of Mr Chick at Pyrford Court, who gave me cuttings of this as well as a photinia. Many of the hostas came from Penny Hobhouse, and the cistus grown from seed collected in Corfu reminds me of walking in the hills of that island on a hot autumn day.

❧ ❧ ❧

The next, or middle, section of the border originally had four *Chamaecyparis lawsoniana* 'Fletcheri', grown from cuttings, as the semicircular backdrop. They grew too tall and wide, so in 1992 we took out two of them and also trimmed the lower branches of the remaining two. This gives us more planting space and casts less shade. We tried to keep this section of the border to a scheme of blue, purple and green – Gertrude Jekyll's influence – but I soon realized we needed more colour here. We added the American beauty bush, *Kolkwitzia amabilis*, and *Campanula lactiflora* 'Loddon Anna' for pink to make a statement with self-sown aquilegias, and

I enjoy the *Thalictrum aquilegiifolium* together with the scented dame's violets or sweet rocket. Spring has tulips – red to echo those under the laburnum, and yellow in the golden section – with pachyphragma and hellebores.

It is worth walking here all through the year to enjoy the *Photinia × fraseri* 'Red Robin', the *Viburnum henryi* from Mr Chick's cuttings and the roses David Austin gave me more recently. The pale mauve lilac, the weigela and the *Viburnum × burkwoodii* were all cuttings from a garden I helped with.

❧ ❧ ❧

The next section, I decided, should have a golden theme; large elms nearby made it very shady and yellow and gold would lighten it up. When the elms succumbed to Dutch elm disease, the border benefited greatly. My semicircle of evergreens were cuttings of *Chamaecyparis lawsoniana* 'Stewartii' and *C.l.* 'Lane' that we had bought in 1960 for the wilderness. By 1969 the cuttings were 90 centimetres/3 feet tall – just right for my design.

In front on one side was a white lilac and on the other a golden privet with *Clematis alpina* climbing through it. Two bought-in trees are the golden elm, *Ulmus* 'Dicksonii', and *Gleditsia triacanthos* 'Sunburst' (syn. *G. t.* 'Inermis Aurea'). On advice from Christopher Lloyd we prune the gleditsia severely each spring so that it will not make too spreading a canopy. I am forever grateful that the golden elm was not affected by disease. An annual prune is essential to keep it shapely; it must not spread or become too tall while the border has bulbs and herbaceous plants to create the right atmosphere. I am amazed at the *Viburnum opulus* 'Roseum', which now towers right above the old cooking apple tree and looks spectacular in flower in April. *Ilex × altaclerensis* 'Lawsoniana' is a central feature, important both in summer and winter.

As always, I try to keep the corners of the beds well planted – the one nearest the fountain often has a change. *Spiraea* 'Arguta', kept to no more than 90 centimetres/3 feet, has *Clematis* 'Proteus' growing through it. *Spiraea japonica* 'Goldflame' has brilliant leaf colour, angelica seeds itself and *Astrantia major* spreads liberally. A talking point in September, at the same time as *Crocosmia masoniorum*, are the first of the snowdrops, *Galanthus reginae-olgae*; they seed and increase gratifyingly in our good border soil, and we explain that a garden can have snowdrops right through until February.

I planned the trees and shrubs in the broad border so that if one day a future owner decided to make it less labour intensive, he or she could take out the interplanting perennials and have either mown or meadow grass, creating a wilderness to wander through.

One of my favourite aspects of the broad border is the narrow strip between the semicircles of evergreens and the castellated hedge at the back. Paving stones were laid here and as I wander through this secret green alley I always have a satisfying feeling of privacy.

❧ ❧ ❧

Rubus phoenicolasius Japanese wineberry

Tropaeolum speciosum

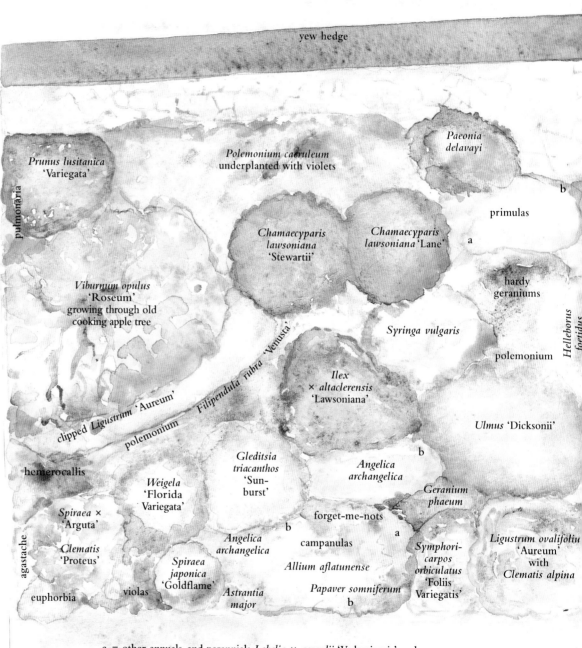

yew hedge

pulmonaria

Prunus lusitanica 'Variegata'

Polemonium caeruleum underplanted with violets

Paeonia delavayi

b

primulas

a

Chamaecyparis lawsoniana 'Stewartii'

Chamaecyparis lawsoniana 'Lane'

hardy geraniums

Viburnum opulus 'Roseum' growing through old cooking apple tree

Syringa vulgaris

Helleborus foetidus

polemonium

clipped *Ligustrum* 'Aureum'

Filipendula rubra 'Venusta'

Ilex × altaclerensis 'Lawsoniana'

polemonium

Ulmus 'Dicksonii'

hemerocallis

Gleditsia triacanthos 'Sun-burst'

Angelica archangelica

b

Weigela 'Florida Variegata'

Geranium phaeum

Spiraea × 'Arguta'

forget-me-nots

a

Clematis 'Proteus'

Angelica archangelica

b

campanulas

Symphori-carpos orbiculatus 'Foliis Variegatis'

Ligustrum ovalifoliu 'Aureum' with *Clematis alpina*

agastache

Spiraea japonica 'Goldflame'

Allium aflatunense

euphorbia

violas

Astrantia major

Papaver somniferum

b

a = other annuals, and perennials *Lobelia × gerardii* 'Vedrariensis' and *Tropaeolum speciosum*
b = bulbs (including *Galanthus reginae-olgae* and yellow tulips)

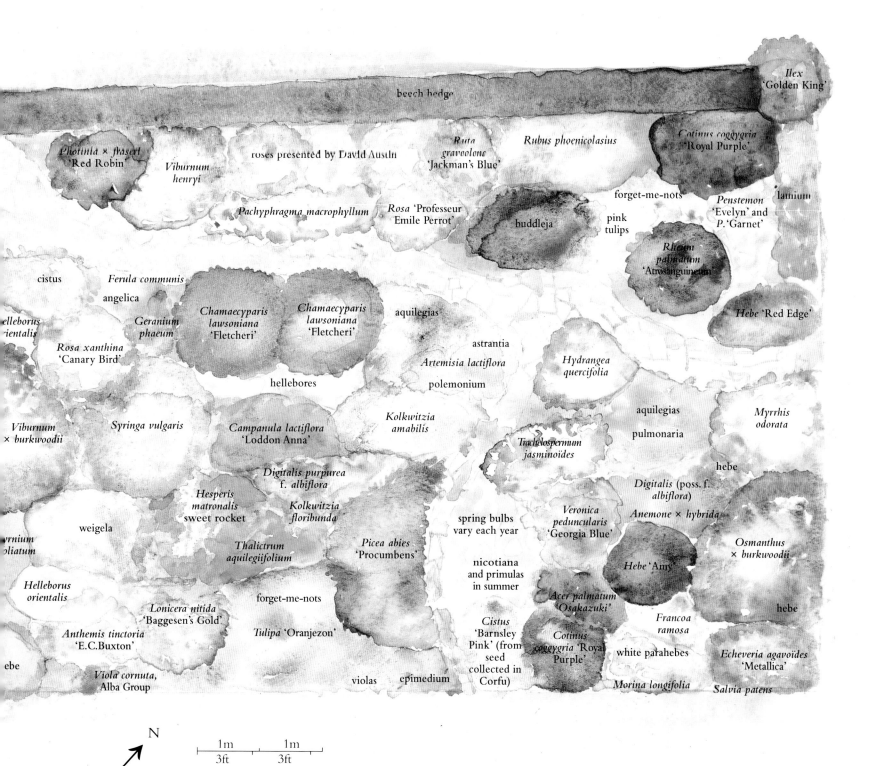

Ilex 'Golden King'

beech hedge

Photinia × fraseri 'Red Robin'

Viburnum henryi

roses presented by David Austin

Ruta graveolens 'Jackman's Blue'

Rubus phoenicolasius

Cotinus coggygria 'Royal Purple'

forget-me-nots

lamium

Pachyphragma macrophyllum

Rosa 'Professeur Emile Perrot'

buddleja

pink tulips

Penstemon 'Evelyn' and *P.* 'Garnet'

Rheum palmatum 'Atrosanguineum'

cistus

Ferula communis

angelica

Geranium phaeum

Chamaecyparis lawsoniana 'Fletcheri'

Chamaecyparis lawsoniana 'Fletcheri'

aquilegias

astrantia

Artemisia lactiflora

polemonium

Hydrangea quercifolia

Hebe 'Red Edge'

helleborus orientalis

Rosa xanthina 'Canary Bird'

hellebores

aquilegias

pulmonaria

Myrrhis odorata

Viburnum × burkwoodii

Syringa vulgaris

Campanula lactiflora 'Loddon Anna'

Kolkwitzia amabilis

Trachelospermum jasminoides

hebe

Digitalis purpurea f. *albiflora*

Digitalis (poss. f. *albiflora*)

Hesperis matronalis sweet rocket

Kolkwitzia floribunda

Veronica peduncularis 'Georgia Blue'

Anemone × hybrida

Osmanthus × burkwoodii

weigela

spring bulbs vary each year

Hebe 'Amy'

viburnum foliatum

Thalictrum aquilegiifolium

Picea abies 'Procumbens'

nicotiana and primulas in summer

Acer palmatum 'Osakazuki'

hebe

Helleborus orientalis

Lonicera nitida 'Baggesen's Gold'

forget-me-nots

Cistus 'Barnsley Pink' (from seed collected in Corfu)

Cotinus coggygria 'Royal Purple'

Francoa ramosa

white parahebes

Echeveria agavoïdes 'Metallica'

Anthemis tinctoria 'E.C.Buxton'

Tulipa 'Oranjezon'

Viola cornuta, Alba Group

violas

epimedium

Morina longifolia

Salvia patens

hebe

N

1m / 3ft   1m / 3ft

Bold planting and wafting scent

The end of the broad border nearest the frog fountain was very shady until elm disease killed an old tree just over the wall. It was tall and spreading so cast a great shadow here for most of the day. Influenced by our visit to Pyrford Court, I decided the best way to brighten it up was to make this the golden end. First I chose for the semi-circle of evergreens *Chamaecyparis lawsoniana* 'Stewartii' and *C.l.* 'Lane', both with golden-yellow foliage. Soon other colours came in – they had to – as well as green: white and the good chartreuse yellows of spring, then adding a bit of red to the yellow to make a soft tangerine. Inevitably, with my love of the combination of yellow and mauve and also scent, a pale purple lilac was planted towards the back, and to balance this is a white lilac, flowering at the same time in May and June.

'Canary Bird' is one of the earliest roses to bloom (**left**) – we have it hiding behind the mauve lilac and *Viburnum × burkwoodii* (white flowers with a pink tinge). You can't go wrong using these time-honoured

favourites. Self-seeders will creep in and you must control their enthusiasm so they do what you, not they, want. Here angelica is welcome, but the moment before the seeds ripen and disperse, the flower stems must be firmly cut down.

I like a full stop at the end of a border (**right**). It must make a bold statement, and under and around this you should use detailed planting – a Gertrude Jekyll thought – as you slow down and turn a corner. Here *Spiraea* 'Arguta', the bridal wreath, dominates, and under it the permanent surrounding planting is *S. japonica* 'Goldflame' and *Astrantia major*. Different ideas can be integrated with these each year; in the picture are primula seedlings, Jacob's ladder and *Helleborus foetidus*. Over the path and growing under the wall are *Ligularia* 'Desdemona', in front of the ivy *Hedera colchica* 'Sulphur Heart'. Our English hellebore, *H. foetidus*, marked the corner all through the winter months, and now in April it waits to drop its ripe seeds around.

Individual moments

Detail in the garden is all-important. In May pause awhile to enjoy the mantle of blue *Clematis macropetala* wrapped around the golden privet (**far left**). Notice the yellow violets, self-sown at the feet of the privet, which follow on from the chionodoxas.

The *Viburnum opulus* 'Roseum' has surprised us with its vigorous growth and reliable beauty (**left**). The perfect white balls growing away above the old apple tree are amazing – they bring light to this corner. Blue sky shines through the *Quercus ilex*, probably planted I believe in the 1830s.

Astrantia major spreads by its root system, *Campanula rapunculoides* by seed and roots (**above, left**) – we like to give seeding annuals the freedom to come up as a surprise in a group of perennials and the woundwort (*stachys germanica*) and the pink opium poppy have just appeared, and so has the allium (on the left).

Golden shrubs need either an echo of gold or a colour in harmony in the foreground – blue, mauve, palest yellow (not red), white.

The Lily-flowered 'West Point' tulips (**above, right**) are used in front of *Ilex × altaclerensis* 'Lawsoniana'. These are left in and a few more added each autumn. The spring forget-me-nots contrast with the tulips and new leaves of *Spirea japonica* 'Goldflame'.

129

Leaf shape and colour

For a few days in mid-October the leaves of *Acer palmatum* 'Osakazuki' (**above, left**) become a brilliant purple, red and orange before they fall to make a wonderful carpet.

In June the interesting flowers of *Morina longifolia* open above its thistle-like leaves (**left**). The forget-me-nots will be replaced by *Salvia patens* 'Cambridge Blue', the tender *Hebe* 'Amy' and *Francoa ramosa*.

Hebe 'Red Edge' (**above**) is one of our favourites, the foliage keeping its colour through the year. A hyacinth, a chionodoxa and sweet cicely leaves grow beside it, with the variegated-leaved form of aquilegia.

In mid-May the stately *Rheum palmatum rubrum* is the focal point at one end of the broad border (**right**). We chose the deep pink lily-flowered tulip 'Mariette' and the pale pink 'China Pink' to harmonize with the claret-red undersides of the rheum's large leaves, with a ground cover of forget-me-nots. The foliage of *Cotinus coggygria* 'Royal Purple' echoes this same colour. A wide planting of sweet cicely, *Myrrhis odorata,* covers the ground under the evergreen *Osmanthus* × *burkwoodii*.

The Wilderness

Every garden, I believe, if it is large enough, should have a space where you can walk and sit and feel alone with nature. It should be a quiet and shady place, with mown paths winding between ornamental trees and shrubs, and flowers studding the grass. A wilderness fulfils these requirements. Ours at Barnsley now has a character somewhere between a woodland and a wild flower meadow. It gives me huge pleasure, and as I walk through the trees and shrubs enjoying the delights around me, I can also think back to the early years when all this was just a dream.

My mother-in-law had had herbaceous borders in this south-west corner of the garden, but by the end of the 1940s they were sparsely planted and weed-infested. For some time the area was simply grassed over and became a place for riding ponies, but by the winter of 1960-61 I was ready to begin planting. This was an opportunity to use and enjoy many exciting trees. In the years since arriving here, I had been noting the names of ones we liked as well as contemplating the design of the garden, which was slowly evolving. I was still a learner and felt that choosing trees was a simple way to start; I could then move on with more confidence to the mixed borders.

Each tree can have more than one seasonal moment, and in the rough grass among the daffodils we included those for spring blossom, berries and autumn colour as well as for contrasting shapes and leaf texture, including evergreens for winter interest. High

> There is always Music
> amongst the trees
> in the garden
> But our hearts must
> be very quiet
> to hear it.
>
> Minnie Aumônier

on our list of preferences were species of sorbus; I had noticed specimens in gardens and at shows, and David and I had seen some spectacular berries on the mountain ash in the Forest of Arden one September. My mind was made up: we would have a small collection of sorbus. We also wanted to have cherries, ornamental crab apples, and others as well.

We selected, with advice from Tim Sherrard of Sherrard's Nurseries, the great white cherry, *Prunus* 'Taihaku', *P. sargentii* and *P.* 'Ukon' with wonderful hanging clusters of almost double creamy flowers in April. *Malus tschonoskii* flowers in spring and colours magnificently in October, and through its upright branches we grow the rose 'Wedding Day' for summer interest. Another crab, *M.* × *zumi* 'Golden Hornet', has a profusion of attractive yellow fruits, so heavy by October that the branches become pendulous.

When I had initially been noting trees I liked, I was not always aware of the soil conditions they needed, but many of the sorbus – both mountain ash and Swedish whitebeam – do extremely well on an alkaline soil such as ours. The flowers of *Sorbus hupehensis* later become bunches of hanging pink-tinged berries that transform into small opaque grapes, seldom taken by the birds. Nearby, always a target for migrant birds, is *S. commixta* 'Embley', one of the best on alkaline soil for red berries and autumn colour.

Amelanchier canadensis blossoms with white flowers in April before the leaves appear, and the early autumn blaze of colour on the tree falls overnight to become a crimson carpet under its newly bare branches. Near the amelanchier are the two rowans, *Sorbus* 'Joseph Rock' with yellow berries and *S. sargentiana* with red. I have planted them beside each other specially to commemorate the association between the two people after whom they are named – Joseph Rock, who around 1900 went plant hunting in China for Professor Charles Sprague Sargent, director of the Arnold Arboretum in Boston. This has become one of my favourite corners of the wilderness in autumn. I was advised by Tim Sherrard to plant *S. sargentiana* branching quite low to the ground so that we could enjoy at eye-level the huge clusters of scarlet fruits, burnished leaves and lovely fat sticky winter buds.

Among these trees is planted the slow-growing but most worthwhile *Parrotia persica*; in fact its rate of growth, not upwards but spreading, has surprised me, and it is now almost embarrassing its neighbours. I love the early, inconspicuous red flowers along its bare horizontal branches and the colour of its autumn leaves, spectacular from September until they fall in late October. They turn red, yellow and orange, and look for all the world like gay parrot feathers. On those spring and autumn days I am aware that it is not always the grand spectacles but the small vignettes of beauty that hold my attention. *Cornus mas* is another shrub which now takes up more space than I anticipated; in January the flower buds swell and by February we enjoy the glow of small yellow flowers which open before the leaves along its spreading branches.

The dawn redwood, *Metasequoia glyptostroboïdes*, we were given in 1964 is now at least 12 metres/40 feet tall; it has maintained a perfect cone shape and is a constant talking point with visitors. The metasequoia is deciduous (before the narrow leaves fall in November they turn a remarkable foxy brown) and beside it is the evergreen wellingtonia, *Sequoiadendron giganteum*, planted in June 1966 to celebrate the birth of our first grandson, Robert.

❧❧ ❧❧ ❧❧

Winter shape and colour are all-important. You must always think of white as a positive colour and the arching wands of *Rubus cockburnianus* stand out elegantly all winter, especially when snow is on the ground. The young green stems of *Salix irrorata* are covered with a white meal. Do not touch the stems of either of these, or you will blemish their bloom.

There is *Eucalyptus gunnii*, with an interesting mottled white bark and evergreen grey foliage; it is one of the hardiest of the Australian blue gums, and the glaucous foliage on its young branches is round and much used by florists in their winter displays. The older branches have longer, greener, tougher leaves. Be bold and pollard some of the old stems; you will then have a plentiful supply of young ones to pick for your arrangements. Whatever generation of branches these leaves spring from, when you crush them you will be reminded of the strong smell of the oil of eucalyptus. I would love to plant an avenue of *E. gunnii* in England, as Dame Elisabeth Murdoch has done up her drive in Melbourne, Victoria, but dare not, for fear that in a hard winter some would die and leave conspicuous gaps.

❧❧ ❧❧ ❧❧

There are other grey-leaved trees in the wilderness, including *Pyrus salicifolia* 'Pendula' and a vigorous *Populus alba*, whose leaves, grey on the underside, whisper in the wind. Beside these two is a clump of evergreen *Berberis julianae*; the scent of its spring flowers always takes me by surprise, wafting on the air from an amazing distance. The round-headed whitebeam, *Sorbus aria* 'Lutescens', is another grey delight; in spring the pale leaves are covered on the underside with almost white down, and these are followed by white blossom. In contrast to the sorbus and in a successful partnership is *Acer platanoïdes* 'Goldsworth Purple' and the purple nut, *Corylus maxima* 'Purpurea', these with a background of Canon Howman's 150-year-old yew trees.

For an impact of yellow, *Chamaecyparis lawsoniana* 'Lane' stands out against a background of the dark yew hedges planted in the 1930s. (We gave a U-turn to part of this hedge in 1954 when we dug the swimming pool.) In this same corner of the wilderness I planted three smoke trees – two *Cotinus coggygria* Rubrifolius Group and one *C.c.* 'Royal Purple'. These have leaves of a lovely deep mulberry colour and now, well established, they give a wonderful autumn display with their smoke-like seed heads. Another golden group, of nine *Ligustrum ovalifolium* 'Aureum', catches the eye from the drawing room window.

These are some of the trees and shrubs we chose for the wilderness in those early days after admiring them in other people's gardens. Now, inevitably, I would like to treat a few as chessmen and move them around the board. Looking back over more than thirty years, I become aware of my mistakes, usually made through lack of knowledge and being attracted by and ordering a plant without knowing enough about its character. Carried away by the drama of the group of incense cedars, *Libocedrus decurrens*, at Westonbirt Arboretum, I planted one beside the poplar to create another tall accent and a contrast of green with grey. However, this cedar really needs to be planted in a group of three to make a statement and not surrounded by other shrubs; it is also best in a parkland setting, where its full drama can be seen from a distance. So out it came, leaving a space to be filled by the laxly shaped golden yew, *Taxus baccata* 'Dovastonii Aurea'.

Another mistake was to plant the *Acer pseudoplatanus* 'Prinz Handjery' – dramatic in spring with exciting shrimp-coloured leaf buds and young leaves – much too close to an Atlantic cedar. One of them had to go: eventually we carefully dug the acer and replanted it elsewhere, but it could not manage the move and died.

ᴓᴓ ᴓᴓ ᴓᴓ

As well as the mistakes, there were the disappointments. We ordered *Sorbus aucuparia* 'Beissneri' for its spectacular trunk and after two years realized our plant had been misnamed. The *Ginkgo biloba* has made so little progress over the years that I suspect it must be planted on stony ground. The *Acer griseum*, too, has grown so slowly that it would clearly do better on richer soil, and the golden-leaved catalpa expired several years ago. The wonderful thing about gardening is that there will always be another chance, another year, and when a gap occurs there is the opportunity to introduce a fresh thought.

At one time we planted two *Viburnum plicatum* 'Mariesii', magnificent with their horizontal branches. Sadly they both died a few years ago, and their place has now been taken by the double *Philadelphus* 'Virginal', which complements the white stems of nearby *Rubus cockburnianus*. I am glad I followed the advice of the eighteenth-century garden designers, who always included shrubs and climbers among the trees in their wilderness.

ᴓᴓ ᴓᴓ ᴓᴓ

I love walking through the wilderness at every time of the year. Even January is full of early promise. By late January and early February there are sheets of snowdrops. One of the first jobs Andy did for me, in the early 1980s, was to dig, divide and replant, singly or in very small clusters, clumps of snowdrops. The best time to do this is when the flowers are just going over and the leaves are still strong. Now each year we try to allow a morning for Andy and Anthony to keep on with this task, and I reckon that in ten years' time the whole wilderness will be a carpet of snowdrops – some single and some double. By the time the snowdrops are ready for division, all the daffodil leaves are well above ground, so damage to these later-flowering bulbs can be avoided.

In spring as the leaves begin to open, each tree has an amazing freshness – then the cherries, crab apples and the amelanchier come into flower. It is one of the most exciting moments, with the many drifts of daffodils – some deep yellow, others yellow and cream. The pheasant's-eye narcissus (*Narcissus poeticus* var. *recurvus*) open later. We are doing our best to establish the snakeshead fritillaries: their leaves look like grass and must not be mown down. Allowing their seed heads to ripen means they can increase naturally.

Lately we have experimented with pricking out tree lupins, foxgloves, poppies and verbascums into the grass. We grow these in plugs from seed and I hope they will give the wilderness area a whole exciting new look in midsummer. Camassias and summer bulbs which succeed and multiply in grassland will be planted as well, as soon as the daffodil leaves are showing. If all this succeeds it will become like an exotic meadow garden. Then we will encounter the mowing problem. A trial carried out at Wisley concluded that daffodil leaves can be cut with no ill effect to the daffodils six weeks after their optimum flowering time. For us this means planning our first mowing for the last week in May, which has become our routine – but now we will have to avoid our newly planted annuals and biennials, and also the fritillaries.

After the first mowing of the wilderness, done with a rotary mower, the grass is extremely yellow and straw-like and has little inclination to grow and green up until there has been a good shower of rain. We usually do this mowing in two 'bites', the central area first and then the sides and back two or three weeks later. This may help us solve the problem of how to incorporate our new meadow flowers: they will have to be planted in clumps, probably around the perimeter, in areas that can be left unmown until the autumn.

❧ ❧ ❧

By summer all the trees are in full leaf and maybe the catalpa and tulip tree are in flower. Walking along the closely mown paths gives me a feeling of complete enclosure and privacy, quite different from the rest of the garden. Then autumn colour creeps up – first to turn are *Sorbus commixta* 'Embley' and the top branches of the parrotia, while the cotinus become a deeper, darker purple. The amelanchier becomes a warm red: you must be quick to catch sight of its transient beauty, for almost overnight the leaves will fall.

I love the days when the sun is shining and I can look up and enjoy the clusters of different sorbus berries against the blue sky. The largest bunches are on the *Sorbus sargentiana* – there may be four hundred red berries on each cluster. The yellow berries of 'Joseph Rock' contrast well with the changing colour of the leaves. The birds are misled and destructive towards these, picking them off and leaving them to fall to the ground when they discover that they are not ripe. It is difficult for us humans to appreciate fully the reason why birds take some berries before others. It is not the colour, so I suspect quite strongly that it is, as with apples, their ripeness. We pick and eat our Laxtons before our Russets, so it is reasonable that birds are selective too. *Sorbus vilmorinii* has elegant clusters of fruit – not stolen by the birds – that hang on much longer than the others: they are rose-red at first, gradually changing from deep pink to a rosy pink and white. On our small

tree they are at eye-level, easily seen, and always cause favourable comments. This sorbus is a wonderful small tree of spreading habit, ideal for a small garden with a lime soil; the delicate ferny leaves cast so little shade it could well be used in a mixed border. Mine came together with *S. scalaris*, now 5.5 metres/18 feet tall, as an exciting present from Sir James Horlick, who grew them from seed on his estate on the island of Gigha, in the Western Isles of Scotland. Memories and associations like this enhance my enjoyment of the seasonal pleasures.

There is another corner of the wilderness that comes into its own in October with a mature bush of *Euonymus alatus*. For two or three weeks the leaves become as beautiful as any deciduous shrub in autumn. This causes visitors to walk close to it and to be fascinated by the broad corky wings on the branches. Its neighbour is another natural curiosity, the corkscrew hazel, *Corylus avellana* 'Contorta'. This corner is backed by a group of a good berrying form of evergreen holly, now 4.8 metres/15 feet tall, which makes a fine winter background for a pollarded golden willow, *Salix alba* ssp. *vitellina*. The evergreen hollies are valuable shrubs in winter with shiny, polished leaves, the stems useful for picking even after the berries have gone.

❧ ❧ ❧

A last visual enjoyment of our trees and shrubs in the wilderness is on winter evenings. Walking across the lawn and looking west when the sun is low, the branches of the trees stand out in silhouette, each one with a different character and shape. The white poplars and the tulip tree, both planted in 1961, are the tallest; keeping pace with them, the two 'spires' of the dawn redwood and the wellingtonia beside it look dramatic in the evening light. Perhaps one of my favourite sights is the elegant *Malus toringoïdes* with graceful spreading branches; some winters its small orange-yellow fruits will hang on until the New Year.

The latest additions to the wilderness are two walnuts, *Juglans nigra*, the black walnut, and *J. regia*, the common walnut. These have been chosen by my son Charles, who now owns the house and garden and looks forward to the fruits in years ahead.

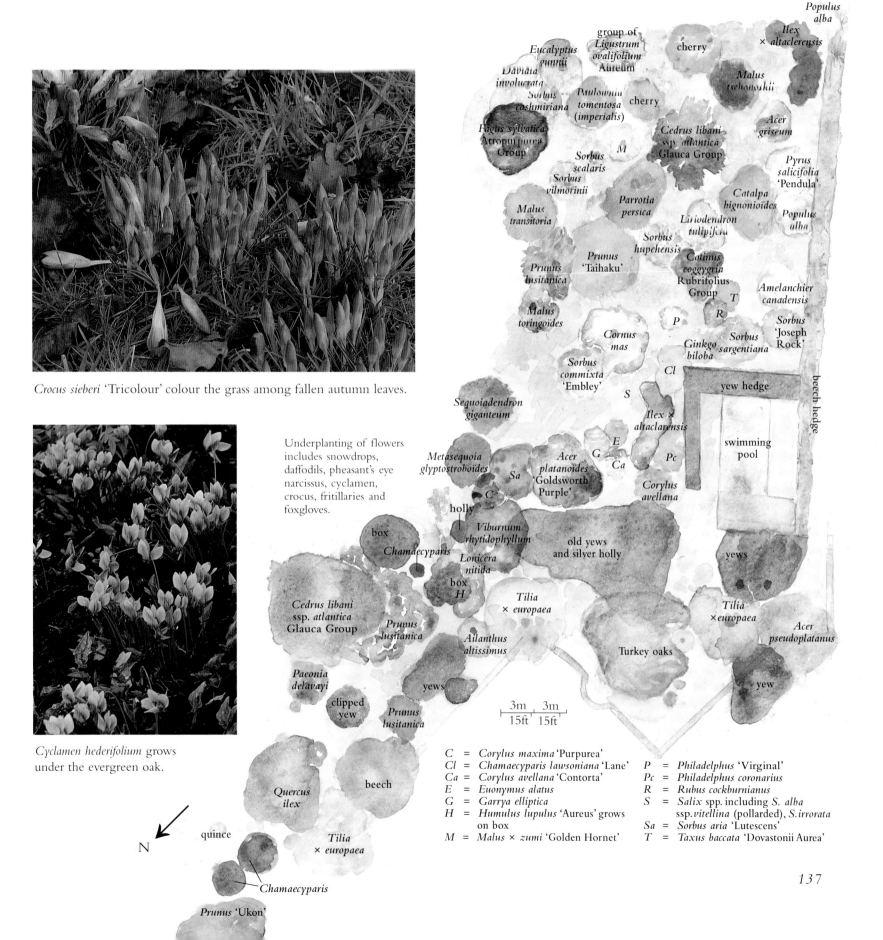

Crocus sieberi 'Tricolour' colour the grass among fallen autumn leaves.

Cyclamen hederifolium grows under the evergreen oak.

Underplanting of flowers includes snowdrops, daffodils, pheasant's eye narcissus, cyclamen, crocus, fritillaries and foxgloves.

Map labels:

Populus alba · Ilex × altaclerensis · cherry · group of Ligustrum ovalifolium Aureum · Eucalyptus gunnii · Davidia involucrata · Malus tschonoskii · Sorbus cashmiriana · Paulownia tomentosa (imperialis) · cherry · Acer griseum · Fagus sylvatica Atropurpurea Group · Cedrus libani ssp atlantica Glauca Group · M · Sorbus scalaris · Pyrus salicifolia 'Pendula' · Sorbus vilmorinii · Parrotia persica · Catalpa bignonioides · Populus alba · Malus transitoria · Liriodendron tulipifera · Sorbus hupehensis · Prunus 'Taihaku' · Cotinus coggygria Rubrifolius Group · T · Amelanchier canadensis · Prunus lusitanica · R · Malus toringoides · P · Cornus mas · Ginkgo biloba · Sorbus sargentiana · Sorbus 'Joseph Rock' · Sorbus commixta 'Embley' · Cl · S · yew hedge · beech hedge · Sequoiadendron giganteum · Ilex × altaclarensis · E · swimming pool · Metasequoia glyptostroboides · Sa · Acer platanoides 'Goldsworth Purple' · G · Ca · Pc · Corylus avellana · C · holly · Viburnum rhytidophyllum · old yews and silver holly · box · Chamaecyparis · Lonicera nitida · yews · box · H · Cedrus libani ssp. atlantica Glauca Group · Prunus lusitanica · Tilia × europaea · Tilia × europaea · Ailanthus altissimus · Acer pseudoplatanus · Paeonia delavayi · yews · Turkey oaks · clipped yew · Prunus lusitanica · yew · 3m 15ft · 3m 15ft · Quercus ilex · beech · N · quince · Tilia × europaea · Chamaecyparis · Prunus 'Ukon'

Legend:

C = Corylus maxima 'Purpurea'
Cl = Chamaecyparis lawsoniana 'Lane'
Ca = Corylus avellana 'Contorta'
E = Euonymus alatus
G = Garrya elliptica
H = Humulus lupulus 'Aureus' grows on box
M = Malus × zumi 'Golden Hornet'

P = Philadelphus 'Virginal'
Pc = Philadelphus coronarius
R = Rubus cockburnianus
S = Salix spp. including S. alba ssp. vitellina (pollarded), S. irrorata
Sa = Sorbus aria 'Lutescens'
T = Taxus baccata 'Dovastonii Aurea'

137

Flowers under trees

The informality of flowering plants allowed to spread under trees is captured in different months, with (**right, above**) an excellent example of how the snowdrops have increased. Those in the foreground are a three-year transplanting and under the beech are four- to five-year-olds.

By April the daffodils have taken over, and looking to the house (**left**), the trunks of the beech and paulownia echo the pillars of the verandah. The paulownia I grew from a seed I picked up from the ground in the Botanic Garden in Padua, so it has a special heritage. Years later when we went back, the Padua tree had gone, so mine has become even more historic.

We planted a golden hop at the feet of the 1830s box bushes (**right**). Each year as it clambers to the top it makes a notable feature, but I am always relieved when the spent stems die down in autumn, allowing the box to regain its own character.

I have mixed feelings towards cow parsley (**far right**). How much should we allow in our wilderness? Its virtue is its lacy beauty, but all the Umbelliferae tribe are difficult to eradicate once established and take over if not controlled. We mow ours down before it seeds and give it only a quarter of the wilderness.

Autumn colour, shape and texture

Two views of the wilderness wearing autumn colour. The tallest tree (**left**), a Norway maple, *Acer platanoïdes* 'Goldsworth Purple', is exceptional when its lime-green flowers open and the young leaves unfurl – at first a reddish brown and later a deep purple. On the right the orange-red fruits of *Sorbus commixta* 'Embley' ripen as the pointed leaflets turn a fiery red. It is one of our best for autumn colour, and the leaves stay on longer than most deciduous trees. In front of it the leaves of *Cornus mas*, the Cornelian cherry, are just turning, while in the right foreground our cotinus have rich plum-purple foliage. They become redder in autumn and 'smoke' well. On the extreme left the leaves of *Sorbus sargentiana* are falling in front of the evergreen *Chamaecyparis lawsoniana* 'Lanei Aurea'.

Three of my favourite trees feature (**right, above**). In the foreground *Sorbus vilmorinii* has discreet clusters of fruit, which start rose-red and as the days go by change to pink and then almost to white. Behind is a spreading branch of *Parrotia persica*, and the background tree is a pale pink fruiting variety of *S. hupehensis*, distinctive throughout the summer for its bluish-green, almost grey foliage, and then in autumn when the fruits show up against the blue sky after the leaves have fallen.

A close-up of *S. vilmorinii* (**far right**) shows graceful leaves, mostly 10-15 cm/ 4-6 inches long, with many pairs of leaflets. Its loose clusters of fruit are in contrast to the tightly packed berries of *S. sargentiana* – there are as many as four hundred (I've counted) in each panicle (**right**). The leaves do their part by turning a brilliant red. In winter the leaf buds, too, are richly coloured red and sticky. To appreciate this small tree fully, it is essential to have a specimen that branches from low down so you have the fruit at eye level.

From autumn into winter

The tulip tree (**below, left**) has distinctive leaves that turn a rich golden yellow by October and hang on through the autumn. The touches of mahogany red in its leaves complement its near neighbours in the garden – the red of the smoke tree and the *Sorbus sargentiana* and the gold of the ginkgo's autumn leaves.

This is a view of the *Sorbus commixta* 'Embley' (**below, right**) looking wonderful silhouetted against a blue October sky. So often in October we get those magical days when there is no wind – an utter stillness – and the the sky is clear blue.

The scene changes dramatically even after a light snowfall (**opposite**). If the temperature is low, snow freezes immediately and will lie along the branches and smallest twigs of the trees and shrubs, weighing them down. The tall evergreen *Eucalyptus gunnii* becomes unfamiliar with its branches, once upright, now pendulous until the sun melts the snow. The beech tree stands with graceful ghost-like branches and snow clusters thickly on the low-spreading *Sorbus vilmorinii*. Enjoy the moment while it lasts.

The Potager

Looking back, I realize it was William Lawson who inspired me to change our vegetable patch from its utilitarian rows of carrots, cabbages, Brussels sprouts, potatoes and leeks into a decorative potager, where, in his words, '*comely borders with herbs*' and '*abundance of roses and lavender [would] yield much profit and comfort to the senses*'. In monastic gardens up to Tudor times, plants were grown in ordered and patterned beds, with flowers specially chosen to decorate the church on Sundays and feast days. Herbs were used for scents and remedies and vegetables were produced for the refectory. One wonders how the housewives managed without the monks' supplies after the cataclysmic events that followed Henry VIII's break with Rome in the 1530s.

Less than a century later, Lawson, a skilful horticulturist and a natural teacher, was living on the southern shore of the River Tees estuary at Ormesby, Yorkshire, where he was vicar for fifty-two years. Not only did he encourage his parishioners to walk in his garden and orchard in the evenings, but he also wrote two charming books, one for the wives and another for the husbands, in 1617 and 1618. I have followed much of his advice, as apt now as it was then. This is from *A New Orchard and Garden*:

'*The Gardener had not need be an idle or lazy Lubber . . . there will ever be something to do. Weeds are always growing . . . Moles work daily, though not always alike . . . In Winter your Trees and Herbs should be lightened of Snow . . .*

'*If you are not able, nor willing to hire a Gardener, keep your profits to your self, but then you must take all the pains; and for that purpose . . . have I gathered these Rules.*'

Everything Lawson writes comes straight from his heart and his own forty-eight years of experience in gardening. Simply and clearly, never teaching too much at one time, he tells of the best medicinal and pot herbs. He instructs how to grow about fifty different herbs, vegetables and flowers, in *The Country Housewife's Garden* commenting:

'*I reckon these only, because I teach my country housewife, not skilled artists....Let her first grow cunning in this, and then she may enlarge her Garden as her skill and ability increase.*'

When I began to garden at Barnsley, Nancy Lindsay gave me the same invaluable advice. She told me to start by growing easy plants so that I would feel pleased with the result – then I could increase my repertoire and expand into rarer and more exotic species.

William Lawson goes on to explain that housewives should have two gardens, one for flowers and the other for vegetables, but the distinction need not be too severe. The flower garden may have herbs growing in the 'squares and knots', and the vegetable garden could include a comely border. I have especially remembered this idea – we have tulips flowering with our early spring lettuces, and hollyhocks and poppies are allowed to seed themselves in strategic places. The eight standard roses 'Little White Pet' are an important central feature. I also use lavender as an edging to line the entrance path instead of the usual box.

Lawson suggests to the housewife that she consider the height of her herbs when she is planting, and place the tallest, such as lilies, hollyhocks, fennel and lovage, by the walls or in the borders. The lowest must be growing in the front. This is perhaps one of the earliest written suggestions about planting a border in a thought-out, artistic manner. However, always practical, it is important to have the beds divided, so that you may go 'betwixt to weed'. I still consider myself to be one of William Lawson's country housewives.

To design my potager I knew I must carefully, slowly, study my patch, keeping Lawson's advice in mind, and considering the virtues of the ground. This has waist-high Cotswold stone walls on the south and west sides; a pity they were not taller, but we were lucky to have them at all. On the north boundary is an old cow shed with a beautiful stone-tiled roof, and on the east a stout post-and-rail fence with a view beyond over ridge-and-furrow grassland. Sometimes I wonder whether a high wall all round would give more protection from icy winter winds and from the hares and moles which find their way in from the fields, but my conclusion is that this plot belongs to the countryside, where I can see my daughter's ponies grazing. At milking time almost a hundred cows come trampling up the lane. The cows are not ours, and it is a nightmare that one day a gate will be left open, but the cowman is careful and our garden visitors seem to be amazed at the sight of warm, black-and-white Friesians streaming past, their milkbags dramatically full. Eventually we erected a homemade trellis screen to run along the inside of this wall for extra wind protection and to prevent the cows from putting their heads over and uprooting anything within reach.

ᐠᗝᐟ ᐠᗝᐟ ᐠᗝᐟ

Nothing in the potager was exactly symmetrical, but fortunately as one lays out a pattern on the ground any eccentricities become unnoticeable. I was comforted by remembering Beatrix Farrand's advice that paths should be laid by eye rather than line, and unless a piece of ground has perfect symmetry, this maxim holds good. No doubt a plan on paper would have come up with a similar

answer to my on-the-spot decisions, but I was much happier standing outside experimenting with the help of bamboos and string.

As you enter the potager, a straight path edged with lavender and standard gooseberries leads to the central feature – an apple tree on dwarfing stock, the branches of which we have festooned (bent) to keep the tree low and pruned into good shapes. Diagonal paths quarter these first two squares and, wishing to emulate La Quintinie at the Potager du Roi at Versailles, I chose four apple trees for the centre of each square to create an element of height, and trained them into goblet shape. They are surrounded by wonderful wedge-shaped industrial bricks which, carefully laid, make a perfect circle.

We acquired these bricks when I heard that a nearby railway station was being bulldozed down and all the rubble taken to make hardcore for a new motorway. My gardener Caroline Burgess and I managed to persuade the demolition contractors to allow us time to collect the most interesting bricks before they scooped them up and away. Our best prize were these wedge-shaped bricks, which had been the 'eyebrows' over the semicircular station windows.

Under the apples on one side are variegated strawberries and on the other alpine strawberries and chives. The beds have their regular rotation of crops, always including salad, roots, brassicas, beans and peas. As these beds make the first moment of impact to the visitor entering the vegetable garden, we devote much thought to deciding on the planting here.

The two quarters beyond the central feature each have four small squares, perfect for growing climbing peas in diagonal form. One bed has a permanent planting of artichokes, and the others are used for quick-maturing lettuce interplanted with cabbages or cauliflowers. The leeks are always interplanted with red lettuce or chicory, and when the peas mature the ground is quickly filled by sprouting broccoli. Onions and lettuce are good companions and the root vegetables, carrots, parsnips and spinach, are sometimes sown in artistic triangles and sometimes in straight rows, as the mood of the moment dictates. We really enjoy the varied colours of cabbages, lettuce and chicory, which look as good in the ground as they do in the kitchen. These beds, about 7 ½ feet or 2.3 metres square, are embraced by L-shaped beds kept primarily for permanent strawberries and are used as seed beds to germinate and grow on our own seedling perennial plants for the pleasure garden.

The raspberries are best grown elsewhere, as the necessary protective netting takes away from the potager's aesthetic pattern. For several years we grew raspberries in a patch 'over the road' from the garden, but this was unsatisfactory, as it was too far to slip out just before supper to gather a picking. Now they are reinstated in the potager, but hidden behind the espalier apples.

ofo ofo ofo

When we were making the main paths we decided they must be broad enough to take a wheelbarrow easily, in fact 70 cm/27 inches wide; the subsidiary paths could be narrower to leave maximum space for the vegetables. To buy all new materials would be more than my budget would stand, so we did it gradually, finding old bricks when buildings were pulled down, and supplementing these with locally made concrete slabs. When the local blacksmith's forge was closed we were allowed the lovely black industrial bricks from that floor. They were perfect to be laid around my two central features. With this success I decided to keep my eyes open for any demolition work which was happening. We needed red bricks to complete the pattern for our paths, and Caroline Burgess and I made several journeys to a brick house which was being demolished in order to make a traffic roundabout. But I was too slow making a decision to buy a wrought-iron front porch to make a decorative archway entrance to the potager. It is always the things you do not do that you regret, seldom the things you do!

The daily routine of the garden had to go on at the same time as path-making, so it all took a long while to complete – several years, in fact. The process was simple, but time-consuming. We dug out 13 cm/5 inches of soil for each path, then laid polythene to prevent perennial weeds coming through, before adding a good 5 cm/2 inch layer of coarse sand. We raked the sand level and trod it firm, then bedded the bricks and blocks into the sand, using a line and spirit level to keep the paths straight and even. No cement was used – it would make the paths difficult to move, and anyway I much preferred the unprofessional look.

ofo ofo ofo

However many different colours and textures you use, a flat piece of ground is usually dull if it has no element of height. This was easy to achieve in summer with pea sticks, bean poles and temporary arches covered with sweet peas, but in winter we could only rely on the roses.

There were two obvious ways of creating instant and permanent height, the essential third dimension – by putting up structures such as trelliswork or arbours, or by planting trees or shrubs, perhaps clipped into shapes, to make individual accents. We began by putting box balls at the corners of each bed and box pyramids whenever we had them available. These all gave me a feeling of definition, and immediately they were in place I was aware of their significance. Even better were the golden privet from the nursery; we chose plants on a single stem so they could be clipped into mophead standards. Now, ten years later, they are an indispensable feature and at only waist height do not cast too much shadow, while giving colour and structure.

I drew out a simple shape for two arbours, easy enough to be homemade. An arbour, or roosting place as it was called in the sixteenth century, needs a seat. We made one from a medieval illustration with the four sides built of bricks, infilled with soil and planted on top with camomile. This never became the success I had envisaged – people just never sat on it. In the end we borrowed white-painted seats from my son Charles and they make a splendid feature in a mainly green garden.

I had longed for an apple tunnel ever since seeing one at Tyninghame in Scotland. Bonham Bazeley of Highfield Nurseries in Gloucestershire asked me to contribute some planting plans for their fruit and herb garden at the Chelsea Flower Show in 1984, and together we worked out a design incorporating an apple tunnel, the structure of which was to be made of metal covered with black plastic. After Chelsea Bonham gave me an eight-arch tunnel, and this now forms an important feature in the vegetable garden, leading on from the central path towards the old cow-sheds. Growing up it are sweet peas, gourds and climbing French beans and runner beans, looking decorative with their scarlet flowers and hanging pods. I suppose one should not grow beans on the same ground each year, so I have tried some new ideas. One autumn at Brooklyn Botanic Garden I saw the Chinese gooseberry, *Actinidia deliciosa* (syn. *A. chinensis*) grown on a pergola. Now we have this, growing well, although I do not expect the English sun to ripen the fruit every year, and to be sure of fruit you must have one male among the females. Bonham also encouraged me to grow Victoria plums on dwarfing stock, festooning the branches. Ideal for a small potager, they are only 1.5 metres/5 feet high, but I sometimes wonder how long a life they will have, tortured as they are into an unfamiliar shape.

To establish the symmetry of this garden we needed a fourth side, so this gave us the wonderful opportunity to plant and train apple trees. I thought of espaliers and then decided that I would like to have an original idea. Instead of simple espaliers, we trained the apple branches to join each other, making arching shapes and a lacework pattern. The grafting was done by Gillian Duckworth using the expertise she had learnt from Wye College. I was later told by a member of the fruit research station that we should have grafted the stems so that the sap made a continuous flow, but we had arranged them so they made a final union. This has been totally successful and I'm glad that – in our ignorance – we did not bow to convention. In spring it makes a lovely screen of apple blossom and in autumn the apple colour is beautiful.

Work in the vegetable garden progresses through the seasons in the same way as in the flower garden. As one crop finishes we add

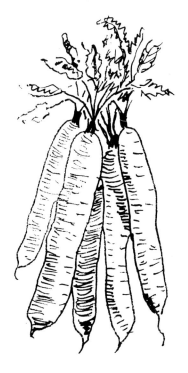

seedlings of another. Lines of carrots can be sown until mid-July, but we must have sown beetroot and parsnips by mid-June or they will not be ready to harvest in time for autumn and winter lunches. Winter cabbage, sprouting broccoli and Brussels sprouts must be planted out where the early peas and beans have been harvested.

Onions will be ripening in July. It takes only a few minutes to bend all the tops in the same direction so that the bed looks neat and tidy. We leave them like this for two weeks and then choose a warm, dry few days to loosen them from the ground so that their bases dry out for another five to seven days. When the moment comes to harvest them, Andy enjoys plaiting them into professional-looking ropes. When first harvested, the onions have a strong taste to them, but they will have lost this pungent flavour by the New Year.

The broad beans we sowed in November will already have been eaten, but the spring-sown ones will be harvested during July and August. It is important to pick them regularly while they are still young and tender. When these are over the old stems are just cut to soil level and the ground is ready, with the nitrogen nodules intact on the bean roots, for planting out all the various brassicas. The dwarf French beans are a favourite, and we sow rows in succession from May to July. We reckon they take sixty to seventy days from sowing until picking, so they coincide with school holidays. The runner beans are an important crop, and with their scarlet flowers they look decorative growing up the archways over the paths.

As autumn moves on there are still plenty of home-grown vegetables to enjoy and salad crops to be harvested, but it is the leeks, onions, parsnips and carrots that carry us through the cold months. Best of all are the Brussels sprouts; these are pricked out during the summer in the beds where we had grown peas and beans. As the sprouts are finishing there will be wonderful purple-and-white sprouting broccoli to enjoy. So the seasons progress, until the spring vegetables come into their own once more.

Just as in the flower garden, things inevitably change in the potager. The eight original standard gooseberries we put in on either side of the main entrance path are now reduced to two. Their mopheads had become too heavy – our fault, I feel sure, for not pruning them severely enough, and with the weight of the fruit several branches broke. I am in two minds whether or not to replace the last two. Growing them as standards certainly makes picking much easier – no bending – and also they add to the overall design. If we decide to replace them (maybe only two or four) we'll have to make sure we prune them better.

Each side of this entrance path the lavender edging is marvellous in summer when it is in flower, attracting hundreds of bees. We replace these bushes every three years. This is now a routine and we take hundreds of cuttings in August or September which will have rooted by spring and be grown on for another year before they are ready to make a new low edging. We have three different varieties, the dark purple 'Hidcote', the paler but stronger scented 'Munstead', and a good pink.

One December night, disaster struck. We had had frosty days so the ground was hard, and this was followed by heavy rain. Water lying in the hollows of the ridge-and-furrow paddock eventually made a stream flowing beside the wall on the south side of the potager, and must have undermined the foundations. It was quite a shock when I went to pick Brussels sprouts to find the wall had collapsed on top of all our nerines, as well as *Rosa* 'Veilchenblau', *R*. 'Mrs Oakley Fisher' and a white rambler. All the small plants growing out of the cracks at the top were in disarray on the ground and had to be salvaged. Nothing could be done before Christmas, but then Colin Feltham, an experienced stone waller, came to the rescue. His beautiful wall, with a good planting space left at the top, will last for years – much longer than a wooden fence – and requires no maintenance. Miraculously, the roses bounced back when they were released from the fallen stones and most of the nerines recovered as well.

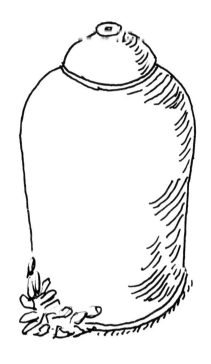

Recently the gardeners and I have made two enlightening visits to Ryton-on-Dunsmore, the Henry Doubleday Research Association organic garden in Warwickshire. The head gardener, Bob Sherman, showed us so much as he took us round that it made me really regret that I had not been there years ago. I was interested in the demonstration patches showing different methods of clearing ground without weedkiller, and it was brought home to me how important it is to collect rainwater – so much softer and purer than tap water – to use in our greenhouse. Perhaps the most useful knowledge we gained on our first visit to Ryton was the value of comfrey leaves. Now we have several plastic barrels which we keep filled with these leaves and topped up with rainwater. The liquid which eventually comes from these is rich in potash and extremely good to use on all pot plants and tubs. We have so much comfrey growing naturally around here that in spring and summer we can make generous use of the fresh leaves as green manure in the trenches prepared for our beans and peas. Our second visit to Ryton we spent learning about winter pruning of fruit trees, worth many hours of learning from a book – again, what a pity not to have discovered this years ago.

❧ ❧ ❧

We all spend time wondering about the future of our gardens – how will they look in years to come? In my own potager, instead of worrying, I try to enjoy the present and look back to William Lawson for inspiration. He wrote that when we walk in our garden in the evening, all our senses should 'swim with pleasure'. So each evening, as I go to cut salad, asparagus, artichokes or mundane cabbages (cooked with the right herbs they can become delectable), I find something to enjoy in every corner of this peaceful, bountiful enclosure.

Design and planting

To reach the potager from the main part of the garden, you pass through the iron gate in the old Cotswold stone wall and cross over a rough track, where the neighbouring farmer's friesian cows may be ambling along to their milking parlour. This immediately changes the feeling: now you are truly in the countryside, where ponies graze on the ridge-and-furrow pastureland, and coming upon the enclosed, decorative and orderly arrangement of crops and flowers is a delightful surprise.

Completing a tour of the garden, the ornamental potager (**above**) is the last pleasure ground to visit. A vegetable garden can be just long lines of cabbage and carrot, but our small area, about the size of a tennis court and its surround, has been divided by

paths into symmetrical patterns. Permanent features create an element of height, with carefully trained fruit trees, standard roses and golden privet. Twin arbours, with seats to relax in, are planted, one with a grapevine and the other with a golden hop. Box edging defines the beds; within them the positioning of the vegetables is carefully thought out, but always having in mind a strict rotation of crops – peas and beans followed by brassicas and then root vegetables. Salad crops, lettuce of every sort, are arranged wherever they can make exciting colour combinations.

I made the basic design of the paths and beds many years ago, and this, with the framework of trees and shrubs, is permanent. Within the beds, though, the planting changes from year, but every season we try to have different patterns and colour effects.

g = standard gooseberry
r = standard rose 'Little White Pet'
vp = victoria plum
gp = golden privet
C = *Crataegus laevigata* 'Rosea Flore Pleno'
a = trained apple
p = trained pear
o = box balls or pyramids
l = pink lavender

All beds are edged with box, parsley, alpine strawberries or lavender.

standing ground for plants for sale

hardwood cuttings

ground for new raspberries

under the arches: *Rudbeckia* 'Marmalade', nasturtiums and marigolds

C

C

C

edging of *Artemisia abrotanum*

perennial phlox

asparagus bed

C

C

C

C

autumn-fruitin raspberries

N

1m
3ft

1m
3ft

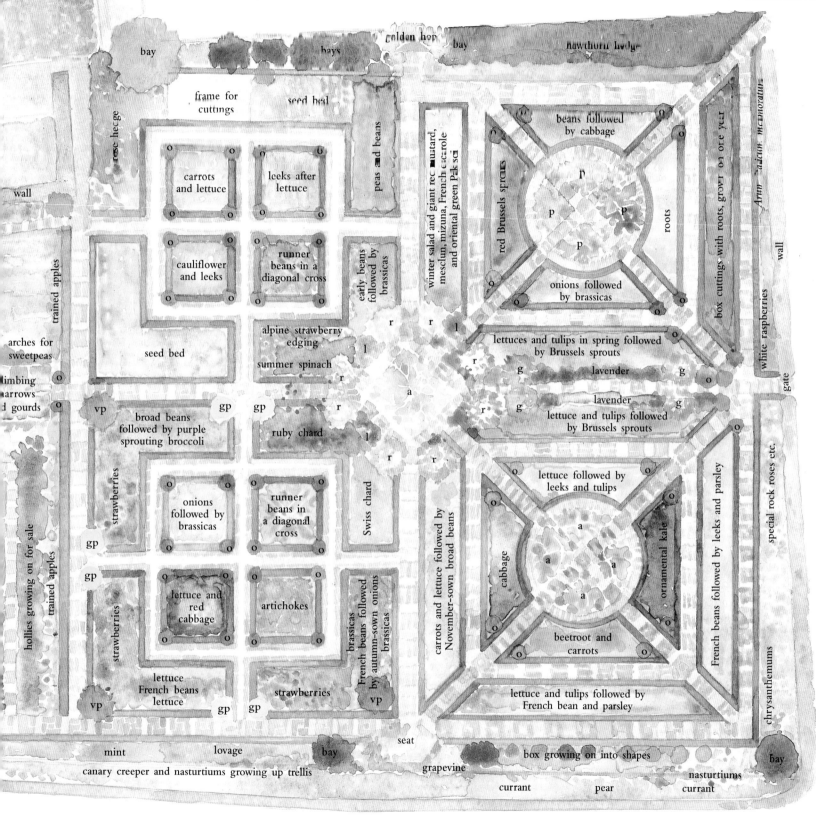

bay

hays

golden hop

bay

hawthorn hedge

frame for cuttings

seed bed

rose hedge

wall

carrots and lettuce

leeks after lettuce

peas and beans

cauliflower and leeks

runner beans in a diagonal cross

early beans followed by brassicas

trained apples

arches for sweetpeas

climbing marrows and gourds

seed bed

alpine strawberry edging

summer spinach

winter salad and giant red mustard, mesclun, mizuna, French escarole and oriental green Pak soi

red Brussels sprouts

beans followed by cabbage

p

p

p

p

roots

box cuttings with roots, grown on one year

Arum italicum 'marmoratum'

wall

white raspberries

gate

onions followed by brassicas

lettuces and tulips in spring followed by Brussels sprouts

r

r

l

r

l

a

r

lavender

g

g

vp

gp

gp

broad beans followed by purple sprouting broccoli

ruby chard

r

l

lavender

lettuce and tulips followed by Brussels sprouts

r

g

g

strawberries

r

r

lettuce followed by leeks and tulips

special rock roses etc.

gp

onions followed by brassicas

runner beans in a diagonal cross

Swiss chard

carrots and lettuce followed by November-sown broad beans

a

a

cabbage

ornamental kale

French beans followed by leeks and parsley

gp

strawberries

hollies growing on for sale

trained apples

lettuce and red cabbage

artichokes

brassicas followed by autumn-sown onions

a

a

vp

lettuce French beans lettuce

gp

gp

strawberries

vp

beetroot and carrots

chrysanthemums

lettuce and tulips followed by French bean and parsley

mint

lovage

bay

seat

box growing on into shapes

bay

canary creeper and nasturtiums growing up trellis

grapevine

currant

pear

nasturtiums

currant

151

Paths and structure

William Lawson, my chief source of inspiration for the potager, was a seventeenth-century gardening clergyman whose knowledge came from practical experience. His emphasis on using paths to divide up the plot into narrow beds, so the 'weeder women' need not tread on the soil, appealed to my sense of design and order: with a free hand in planning our vegetable garden I could enjoy making patterns with the paths, deciding their width and surface – I had set my heart on old bricks and paving. When I drew out the design on squared paper and calculated the bricks and paving required, I was surprised by how much the paths would reduce the growing space for

vegetables. I reduced the width of some of the subsidiary paths from 70 cm/27 inches to 45 cm/18 inches – wide enough to work from but too narrow for walking abreast. Then we set about scavenging old bricks – not easy in stone country. Slowly we came upon them, from an old barn, the blacksmith's shop and a redundant railway station. I bought concrete paving slabs locally, always waiting for enough slightly imperfect cheaper slabs to make a reasonable load.

The pattern of the paths vary and this, as well as the way in which we laid them without cement, gives informality within a formal design. Each path has a 'living' edge to prevent soil from straying and to add definition. We use various species of box, lavender and even alpine strawberries to edge the paths.

In spring, the apple blossoms bring bees to pollinate the trees and this heralds the productive months in the potager.

The beds: shape
and plant patterns

By planning simple geometric shapes for the beds (see pages 150-1) I aimed to get away from the traditional kitchen-garden layout of rows of vegetables stretching across the garden. Some beds are square, embraced by 'L' shapes, while others are long and narrow and surround a circular motif.

Each spring when Andy and I are making our vegetable planting plan, we think first of the seasonal rotation of crops – pulses (peas, beans), followed by brassicas (cabbages, cauliflowers), followed by root crops (carrots, parsnips). For decorative effect lettuces and other salad greens are always planted as short-term crops alongside the main crop.

Although I love the spring, when everything is young and fresh and each day brings new excitement, I also enjoy the summer months when the potager is full of exuberant colours and an abundance of vegetables. I love going out in the evening to pick just three vegetables – perhaps peas, cabbage and spinach, or potatoes, french beans and courgettes – which I cook and eat separately, sprinkled with a single herb. Three simple courses become a gourmet meal.

In the farther bed (**above**) is the last of the sprouting broccoli, a crop that continues from early spring right through until the beginning of summer. We love to keep the ground well covered: a bed of early lettuce is under-planted with tulips, and young cabbages are interplanted with more lettuce.

The narrow beds provide a delightful spectacle in May (**right**), when ranks of pale yellow tulips contrast with spring vegetables, broad beans and lettuce. Now is the moment when the apple blossom is at its best, and the central festooned apple tree attracts scores of bees as well as the human eye. Visual interest, especially colour, above ground level is important in the vegetable garden, along with scent – in addition to productivity.

The attractive effects of leaf contrast are exploited throughout the potager. Purple lettuce (**far right**), to be harvested in midsummer, is grown alongside parsley that is consumed throughout the year, and leeks, which will be harvested in the autumn.

Contrast and plenty

The fun of planning what to plant in the potager is endless. There are two major considerations. It must look attractive, with colour contrasts of vegetables, and we must always have plenty to cut.

When planting for plenty, it is essential to think about harvesting. Lettuces need less time to mature than leeks, cabbages and cauliflowers, so you can plant them as temporary infillers while the other crops grow. This also has the advantage of keeping the beds well covered. During hot, dry summers well-filled beds help to keep the ground from drying out and baking.

Study the seed catalogues to find the best selection of lettuce varieties to carry you through many months and make wonderful contrasts of greens and reds. The beds shown here are filled with a succession of crops arranged decoratively. The pattern of alternating rows of 'Ruby' and green 'Little Gem' lettuces (**above**), the red row interspersed with later cauliflower, yields quick crops. Brilliant golden box (**right**) edges rows of 'Rouge Grenoblois' and then 'Salad Bowl' lettuce with 'Ruby Ball' cabbage for autumn eating. As well as 'Tom Thumb' and 'Lollo Rosso' lettuces and 'All the Year Round' cauliflowers, the bed (**far right**) has onions and leeks, all bounded by box.

Structure and height

The area of the kitchen garden beyond the apple screen and the old cowsheds used to be a no-man's land. Because of its position, it had been left out of the overall plan, but when Bonham Bazeley of Highfield Nurseries gave me an Agriframes 'apple tunnel', this seemed the obvious place to put it.

The tunnel creates a perfect entrance when you enter the potager from the cowshed end (**left**). Apple trees have never grown on its arches – instead we put on a different show of annuals each summer. We always have sunflowers – I love the way they peer over the top, and as soon as the seeds ripen the birds love them too. For several years we have grown *Rudbeckia* 'Marmalade' along each side, and last year we grew annual marigolds too. Nasturtiums are encouraged to grow up the frame, and they soon wind their way around the sunflower stems. As we usually have a surplus of lettuce seedlings we plant them along each side of the path. It seems a shame to take them out when they start to bolt, so we allow them to remain (these are 'Rouge Grenobloise') as a good dark foil to the nasturtiums. A clump of golden feverfew in the left foreground probably seeded itself, and beyond it a stem of *Actinidia deliciosa* has twirled to the top of the nearest arch.

The arbour (**right**) was photographed shortly before an autumn gale blew it over. Fashioned by Andy, its structure, trelliswork made from narrow battens, is in fact very simple.

By the end of summer the golden hop completely envelops it, smothering it with clusters of hops that I use for autumn flower arrangements. It is a peaceful place to sit and contemplate and you can understand why, in the sixteenth century, such arbours or bowers were called 'roosting places'. We allow some of the long shoots to trail gracefully over the ground; these, if given a covering of soil, will take root and make new plants to sell in the nursery.

In front of the arbour is the bed we devote to sowing seeds from the perennials and annuals we have saved. Here, poppies and foxgloves have taken over and we try to keep the best colours, by removing the less attractive ones. The orange Welsh poppy, *Meconopsis cambrica*, in its double form, is scattered through this plot. Seed sowing teaches great patience. Some seeds germinate almost overnight, others wait until their hard cases have opened, while some wait until the conditions – moisture, temperature and day length – are just right.

Vertical colour

The camera has captured a moment (**below**) when we ourselves may have been too busy to pause. The pure white of the sweet pea, *Lathyrus odoratus* 'Swan Lake' enlivens the bright red and yellow of the mixed trailing nasturtiums.

The yellow single hollyhocks (**right**) are grown from seed given to me by American garden designer Ryan Gainey, which came originally from Monet's garden at Giverny.

Andy Bailey built this bamboo framework (**left**) for beans to climb up and have plenty of light. We like the effect of the squares of golden box used as edging for beds where the scarlet flowers of runner beans or the mauve hues of purple cabbage grow – both colour and structure make a dramatic contrast.

'Laxton's Fortune' apples are carefully trained along the 'screen' (**below**) where yellow-flowered nasturtiums have been allowed to thread their way along the apple branches.

A flowery look

'… it is meet that we have two Gardens; a Garden for flowers and a Kitchin-garden…not that we mean so perfect a distinction, that we mean the Garden for flowers should or can be without herbs good for the Kitchin, or the Kitchin-garden should want flowers.'

William Lawson's words made me realise how important it would be to give my potager a flowery look, especially in the spring, when the plum, apple and pear trees are in bloom.

The variegated strawberries that grow as ground cover under the goblet apple trees

have tulips planted through them (**above**), adding elements of colour and height. Sometimes we keep to one colour scheme, at others we add new tulips – here a deep pink tulip mingles with the lovely Lily-flowered *Tulipa* 'White Triumphator'. Spring has a quality of freshness, and in this picture the ephemeral beauty of the tulips and blossom contrasts with the established structure – the paving, the apple trunks and, especially, the full, dense, rounded box balls.

I vividly remember standing in our new vegetable patch trying to calculate by eye which exact spot should become its central point, for from here the pattern of paths was laid. For several years a metal urn marked this

spot and then not long ago we planted an apple tree, which I decided must have its branches festooned. Around this young tree (**right**), we have planted narcissus for spring, and then the various lavenders come on. I have also planted out an unusual upright box, now nearly 1.2 m/4 feet tall and ready for a new home in the main garden.

The beautiful pink lavender (**far right, above**) flowers in the centre square of the potager beside the paths. *Viola* 'Bowles' Black' has been allowed to seed through it, the mauvish-pink, dark purple and gold tones drifting in a chiaroscuro of colour harmony, and (**far right, below**) between the cabbages and alpine strawberries.

Wall cover, edgings and infills

When this dry stone wall (**above, left, centre** and **right**) collapsed in 1993, the roses were buried under fallen stones for two to three weeks, but surprisingly they recovered once trained back to the rebuilt wall. The eye-catching mauve-blue rambler *Rosa* 'Veilchenblau' must have a well-established root system, for it never looked back, while the 'Iceberg' rose, less well established, took longer to produce

productive growth. *Meconopsis cambrica*, an energetic self-seeder, also survived.

The same low wall provides a first view of the potager (**above, right**) from the path by the tennis court. Here (and also **above, left**) *Rosa* 'Veilchenblau' is in bloom.

The dramatic dark purple *Lavandula* 'Hidcote' (**far left**) is our chosen edging plant in much of the potager. To keep it in good shape and looking tidy, you should clip it back after flowering, and then again in spring to remove old growth and allow new growth to take over. The leaves of this lavender are very strongly scented while the flowers of *L.* 'Munstead' are the most

fragrant. Self-sown borage and red lettuces allowed to bolt give a varied colour scheme.

This bed (**centre, left**) uses alpine strawberries as edging and the variegated-leaved strawberry is effective both visually and as a groundcover under our goblet apples. It flowers well, but the fruit is sparse and disappointing.

Beside the box balls, *Viola* 'Bowles' Black' is brought to effective use as edging (**left**). Elsewhere we allow 'Bowles' Black' and *V. labradorica purpurea* (now *V. riviniana* Purpurea Group) to seed themselves. They pop up between box balls and in the beds, and young plants are always in demand in the selling yard.

The Courtyard and Conservatory

I love to walk straight from my sitting room and be surrounded by flowers and scent. This was easy when I lived in the main house for there were borders right up to my door. Now, the atmosphere is different – my small courtyard has paving and lots of tubs and I always have something special for those who appreciate detail – the flowers on the sarcococca, the emerging hellebores, moss between the paving, the purple berries on the billardiera. Most important are the tubs by my study door, which I go through ten or twenty times a day: the nearer you are to your 'home base', the more interesting the planting should be. I try to keep my courtyard area simple but effective in winter, first with *Narcissus* 'Paper White', then with tulips and daffodils, and full of flowers in summer.

Years before the fashionable explosion of 'extra rooms', David and I often discussed building a conservatory attached to the house. Sadly – he would have enjoyed it so much – we never achieved this idea together. When I moved into The Close in 1988 there was a space crying out to be made into a conservatory. It was an untidy no-man's land lying between a high wall and the drawing room of my new house. We put double glass doors leading from my new drawing room into this area. Now all that was needed was a façade and a roof. Charles Morris, a Norfolk architect, designed them. The façade has four stone pillars and three sets of double doors, cleverly positioned so that half of each pillar is visible both inside and out. The roof, made of curved wooden joists and flexible carbonate, is prettily hipped – almost dome-shaped. For the floor, Charles found old malting tiles, most decorative with their

pierced holes, and he incorporated an iron grating from a disused nineteenth-century greenhouse in an underfloor heating system.

Another of my ambitions was to have a grotto. The mossy east-facing wall of the area gave an impression of damp – like a hermit's dwelling. To make a virtue of this (though without the hermit) I decided to incorporate a grotto here. As soon as this was mentioned Simon Verity's natural enthusiasm took hold. We discussed coral, abalones, mussel shells, goldfish, three pools, a trickling waterfall and even a ceiling mirror that reflects our thoughts. Simon constructed the three small pools and with inventive flair began to cover the sides with coral and shells. Then Diana Reynell deftly translated his scheme into an ageless grotto with water trickling and stones and shells sparkling – a unique water feature.

I decided to have one corner of the conservatory as a raised bed where I could sink plants such as arum lilies, ferns and a few pelargoniums. The rest of the space is filled to overflowing with pots, some standing on the stone floor, others on tables so that their beauty is at eye level. There are many pelargoniums, especially *P.* 'Clorinda', now climbing high with its pink flowers forever in bloom. There are sedums, echeverias and fuchsias, hoyas climbing to the roof and a passion flower grown from seed. Above the lowest third pool is a protruding ledge, where we have *Pelargonium* 'Lady Plymouth'. For winter there are *Sparmannia africana* and jade plants, together with the bulbs planted in bowls before Christmas.

From February until April the conservatory takes on another use: it becomes all-important for hundreds of seedlings – lettuces, chicory, early brassicas, tobacco plants, salvias, cosmos and whatever half-hardy annual has caught my fancy this year.

The courtyard in spring and summer

We try to keep the tubs and pots in my small paved courtyard full through the seasons. In February and March the tubs each side of my study door start with crocuses, then have a few 'Paper White' narcissus and a quantity of *N.* 'Parisienne' (**left, above**). As these die down the tulips come into flower. In 1994 we had *T.* 'Fringed Elegance' seen (**left, below**) before the petals open and the fringing is revealed; they were so successful we repeated them again in 1995. For a change we then planted *Narcissus* 'Unsurpassable', a dramatic large-trumpet golden yellow, and these narcissi have stood up well to the vagaries of our weather – wet, cold, sudden sunshine, hail and change of temperature.

I love all narcissus for their scent and freshness. They are the herald of spring.

Penstemons (**above left**) are brilliant in tubs as well as in the border. Here *P.* 'Rubicundus', with a white throat and deep red stem, flowers continuously. Left of the tub, bronze fennel and euphorbia have seeded themselves beside my study door.

Lavatera 'Barnsley' (**above right**) seen through the lacy leaves of a self-sown fennel. The lavatera flowers open white with their dark centre, and change slowly through pale to deeper pink as they develop.

169

My indoor garden

Look carefully at the detailed stone and shell work of the
grotto (**above**) designed by Simon Verity with the help of
Diana Reynell. Then browse around to enjoy the planting
(**right**). In spring this room is an extra greenhouse, and in
summer it becomes my 'tidy' room for entertaining. In winter
it is kept frost-free for special plants. The pelargonium on the
table was given to me by Charlie Hornby, and in the corner
P. 'Compton's Delight' never rests, flowering from late winter.

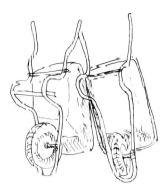
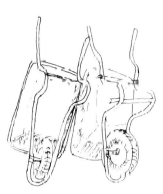

Work and Maintenance Through the Year

'How many people look after the garden?' is the question I am always being asked. My answer is 'four and a half', not counting myself. I have come to this figure as an average over recent years: some days in summer there are as many as six people working in different places; some winter days there will be three, and once a week – usually Tuesdays – Les and Andy used to work alone, feeling relaxed and free to get on with their own jobs uninterrupted.

When David and I came here in 1951, my father-in-law's head gardener, Arthur Turner, was in sole charge. He and I had a friendly relationship, although we never discussed seed sowing (which I felt was his province) or aesthetic ideas – perhaps a legacy of the Edwardian tradition between owner and gardener. When it became impossible for Arthur Turner to grow all the vegetables and keep the ornamental gardens to a high standard single-handedly, he was helped by Charlie Beeks, who retired to one of our cottages and devoted his spare time to digging, sweeping and tidying. Then Arthur's brother-in-law Fred Willis came along and helped with the vegetables. Andy acknowledges how much he learned about vegetable gardening from Fred.

New challenges came in the 1960s, when we were encouraged to open to the public for the National Gardens Scheme – one Sunday a year at first. This was a great incentive to weed, clip and mow. Cecil Tomblin, who was on hand at the time, was immaculately tidy, and his example taught me an enduring lesson. It was also he who installed my mist propagator in 1963; soon we had a

Home-made frames cover young plants for winter protection and bags of compost anchor them from strong winds.

surplus of plants, which started the ball rolling for plant sales. And more plants to look after meant more helpers.

I have always been lucky to have people asking to work here. Sometimes they are local people, sometimes college students or others who have great skills. They may not plan to stay long, but even a summer can be enough time for them to learn and to give us fresh ideas. Since Arthur Turner's retirement in 1975, the gardeners and I have worked much more as a team. I find it is very important to arrange the work programme so that the right job is allocated to the right person. To get the best results, gardeners should not feel that their work is monotonous, so they must be given the chance of a change occasionally.

❧ ❧ ❧

There was Caroline Burgess, who first came to Barnsley House as a schoolgirl to ride the ponies and do weeding for pocket money. She left school wanting to 'get into gardening', worked here for three years in charge of the flower garden until 1981, then became a student at Kew. A great worker, always meticulous and giving of her best, Caroline is now head gardener for Frank Cabot at Stonecrop in Upper New York State, where she plans to open a school for horticultural students. Gillian Duckworth arrived to work here for a year just after Caroline left. She had completed a horticultural course but lacked practical experience, and David and I were about to set off for four weeks in the USA. I need not have worried: she was wise enough to conjure country wisdom from seventy-year-old Fred Willis and muscle from seventeen-year-old Andy, and managed perfectly with the business of propagating the tender plants and coping with visitors.

At this time John Scarman spent a year here, working and learning; he went on to work with roses at David Austin and then to open his own business, Les Roses du Temps Passé. Then John Clark was head gardener for five years. After he left to work in a large nursery, Andy and Les Bailey gradually took over as joint head gardeners. Andy had come straight from school in 1980, a raw recruit. From the first he and I knew we would get on well together. When his younger brother Leslie left school he too came here, and from then until 1995 they were the mainstay of my garden workforce, Andy in charge of clipping, mowing and the potager, Les taking care of the pleasure garden, propagating and the selling yard. Three days a week, all through the year, Anthony Verey, my grandson, arrives on his motor bike to help the gardeners. Together we are always expanding our knowledge of plants, seed sowing, vegetable growing, clipping, pruning and fertilizing. Most important of all, we realize we must ever be learning.

All sorts of skills are valuable in a garden like this. Besides the head gardeners, we have had a supporting cast of many different characters. Mike Peace was a countryman with an instinct for plants and a knack for noticing when rabbits got in. His great height was another virtue – we always gave him the high-up pruning jobs. Nicholas Lambourn came straight from college and in his year and a half here made good progress with Andy in the potager, removing the fruit cage, laying the paths for the fourth square and putting up trellis. Sue Spielberg and Margie Trevelyan-Clark were both academic in their approach, dovetailing working at Barnsley with their studies; we were lucky to have them, because while they were learning about the practical work, they passed on much horticultural knowledge to us. Rupert Golby, now a sought-after designer and expert on container planting, filled in time here one summer while building up his own landscaping business.

Looking after visitors and organizing plant sales is a demanding aspect of the garden at Barnsley House. Selling plants may sound easy, but it is surprising how many questions come up and how much time you can spend advising visitors on plants for specific sites. Saturdays are always our busiest days, and with no Monday-to-Friday gardeners willing to help, I try to stipulate that learner gardeners must be here on Saturdays. Rachel Churchward, Sheila McCausland and Jilly Dare have all helped, but without the sup-

Purple sage makes a perfect foil for the Crocus vernus *'Jeanne d'Arc'.*

The corners of the borders have a bold planting of Iris reticulata, *allowed to increase every year.*

Species Crocus sieberi *'Violet Queen', flowering in February, has multiplied in our borders.*

port of my son Christopher on summer Saturdays I could never have coped. I owe a great debt of gratitude to Sue le Fleming, who came two days a week for several years to keep the mist propagator full, and to Rosemary Hughes, to whom Sue passed on these skills. Rosemary, now our cuttings expert, takes visitors round and fits in to any role. Maureen Harper has been one of our best helpers, keeping the selling yard impeccably tidy with everything well labelled, and taking infinite trouble with our customers.

Many overseas students write to us wanting work, and I always try to pass their names on to friends if we do not need extra help. Some, like Kelly Horn from Tallahassee and Alex Smith from Atlanta, are studying landscape design and to help them we give them as varied a range of work here as possible, as well as recommending other gardens for them to visit. Barbara Robinson was our most surprising 'student'. Now President of the Bar Association of New York, she really made her mark during her four weeks here. Passionate about gardening, she keenly performed

The magic of cobwebs in winter on a spreading juniper.

every task we gave her and now assures me that her Connecticut garden has been transformed by her experience at Barnsley. I hope that all our other gardeners have been as happy working here; I hope they feel that gardening is not only a career, but a way of expressing their artistic nature, and that owning or working in a garden will always enrich their lives.

I must not forget those other workers, the chickens, who all through the year make our valuable compost. They live in the two pigsty buildings in the car park and have a generous run. Everything from the garden – apart from the wicked weeds like ground

elder and convolvulus – and all the household waste is thrown to them (they also get corn every morning). Whenever they see a wheelbarrow approaching they gather excitedly around the gate of their enclosure and immediately start pecking and scratching, competing for the best pieces. The nitrogen in their droppings helps to convert garden and kitchen waste into valuable soil. The level of their run will rise by a good 60 centimetres/2 feet in twelve months. Then Christopher comes with his front-end loader on a frosty morning when the tractor wheels will not make horrendous marks. The rotted-down waste is taken to a long heap by the chicken run and enclosed by old tracking. Turning it over encourages more breaking down, and by the time it is used on our borders and for potting, it is beautiful soil, containing nitrogen, phosphates and trace elements – all the nutrients our plants require. We do not analyse it, but from experience and results know that it cannot be bettered by any proprietory brand of growing compost.

To make our potting compost, the first stage is to sieve the soil from the pile by the chicken run. We then mix three parts of this with one part of cocoa-shell (for drainage) and one part of recycled peat, which we usually buy from a commercial grower in the form of the previous year's used tomato bags; in this way I am recycling rather than buying newly dug peat. Slow-release Vitax Potting Base is added in the proportion of 1 ounce (about 28 grammes) per bucketful.

Our garden is not strictly organic – we do use systemic sprays in the vegetable garden to combat whitefly – but whenever possible we use organic sprays and fertilizers. On the gravel drive and for the paths in the potager, weedkillers have become indispensable. Today the price of labour makes this vastly more practical than hand-weeding.

Machinery and weedkillers obviously speed up many gardening tasks, but they cannot provide the personal touch which will always be essential in the imaginative garden. Working in the same garden for many years is like getting to know the ways of a friend. Instinctively I now appreciate where the frost lingers longest, where the wind blows hardest, where the earliest bulbs will push through. I also know that although no two years' weather is ever the same, the routine through the seasons always follows a pattern. For this reason, potential gardeners should aim at working at least a full year in one garden while they are learning.

January, February and March

We come back to work after Christmas with renewed vigour. The borders all look neat and the bulbs coming through give a wonderful feeling of expectancy. January, February and March in the garden are a season in their own right. We may imagine that nature is resting, yet there is constant activity below ground, where worms are working and herbaceous plants establishing themselves, making new roots, preparing for the next season's display.

Jobs that yield quick results are the most fun to do. On a sunny day, even if the air is frosty and the ground hard, we always enjoy pruning and tidying the ornamental deciduous trees – sorbus, malus, amelanchier, parrotia and euonymus; the prunus or ornamental cherries are better pruned later when the sap is up. We cut off all crossing branches and try to maintain our trees so that they are pleasing in size and silhouette and have open centres. We look

Clematis cirrhosa *var.* balearica, *a winter joy, flowers for three months on a warm wall.*

inside the conifers and remove any wood that has died; it is surprising how much better they are when this is done. We choose a sunny day for pruning and tying in the laburnum. Even in February the flower buds are fat and distinguishable from the leaf buds. We also make sure that any strong wisteria stems are not strangling the laburnum branches.

All through the winter the glowing red stems along the top of the lime avenue have been spectacular, but these must be cut hard back now. The various *Cornus alba*, if pruned in March, will make wonderful new growth each summer; so will the willows, especially *Salix alba* 'Chermesina' (correctly *S.a.* var. *vitellina* 'Britzensis'), *S.a.* var. *vitellina* itself and *S. irrorata*. Our cotinus all have different treatment. Those in the wilderness, now tall bushes, are left alone. *C. coggygria* Rubrifolius group has last season's growth pruned back at about 1.2 metres/ 4 feet. Another specimen in the front of a border is cut almost to ground level each March and by summer produces splendidly large leaves on 90-centimetre/3-foot wands. We leave the pruning of the grey-leaved shrubs – santolina, shrubby artemisias, sage, rue and lavender – until March, then cut them back. Last summer's growth acts as winter protection against hard frost.

My diaries reveal problems that cropped up from time to time. One year the *Quercus ilex* was looking very sad, having flowered profusely the summer before. I was advised to take up a circle of turf under the farthest spread of the branches and scatter bonemeal there, thus feeding the end roots, and then bore holes and put in dried blood. This worked wonders and revitalized the old tree.

We prune back our old-established apple trees in February or March, before the sap starts to rise, cutting back last season's growth to two fruit buds. The stronger-growing an apple tree, the later you should prune it to reduce its vigour and increase its yield. The climbing roses on the wall are pruned and secured to the wire netting or available nails.

Non-horticultural jobs — administration and maintenance — are a recurrent theme, with variations, on frosty days when snow, rain or wind keeps us indoors. Equipment is cleaned and serviced, frames and tool handles mended, doors painted, potting sheds tidied and garden seats cleaned and repaired. Bottles and packets of chemicals are sorted and those that have lost their potency discarded. Other jobs are sorting out the accumulation of old catalogues, writing labels and scrubbing flower pots and seed trays. We have to keep the greenhouse glass clean to allow in as much light as possible. Days when snow is drifting will reveal which panes need replacing; cracks can be filled temporarily with cotton wool.

The indoor job I like best is to sort and clean the seeds we collected last year and stored in an old refrigerator. In January we put them into envelopes, label them and decide whether they should be planted indoors in trays or outside in seed beds. When we have listed our own seeds, we will know what others we need to buy. Seed sowing in trays is a regular February task on those frosty and unpredictable days when we cannot get on to the soil. Lack of greenhouse space has always been my problem, especially in winter when it is full to overflowing with tender plants like geraniums and fuchsias. However, after our boilers were converted to oil in 1979 and the cellar space cleared of solid fuel, we had fluorescent lights set up, and the regular heat from the boiler keeps the temperature just right for seed ger-

mination. Sowing the seeds is one thing, but it is only the first step in a plant's life: seedlings must be cared for and space found for them after they have outgrown the fluorescent lighting table. We must be wary of the greenhouses becoming overcrowded with fast-growing plants demanding more and more space and light, all waiting for the weather to warm up sufficiently for them to be moved outside or into frames. Now, for a few weeks we add extra tables for seedlings in the conservatory.

Our usual date for sowing early cabbage, lettuce and cauliflowers is mid-February. We stagger the lettuce sowing and usually have six different varieties, ranging from the easy 'Tom Thumb', 'Little Gem' and 'All the Year Round' to the more unusual red and green 'Rubens Romaine', 'Rouge Grenobloise' and 'Merveille des Quatre Saisons'. We also sow ornamental kale and red Italian chicory, 'Rossa di Treviso' and 'Rossa di Verona'. The chicory looks exciting planted as summer bedding between diascias in the flower garden.

Flower seeds like nicotiana and *Salvia patens* which should be in flower by July must have a good start, but *Rudbeckia* 'Marmalade' and *Lavatera* 'Mont Blanc' are much better sown in March; by early June they will be quite large enough to be put into their flowering positions. The same applies to *Nicotiana langsdorffii* and the old-fashioned scented sweet peas.

Each year we sow a selection of different and more exotic plants, and the seeds of those I have brought home from foreign visits. One year it was a wonderful pale yellow hollyhock, which came to me via Ryan Gainey in Atlanta; he had been given it in Monet's garden at Giverny. Now these are allowed to self-sow in the vegetable garden. Seeds of the pretty pink climber *Maurandya*

Early flowers at Barnsley House garden

Anemone blanda, auriculas, bergenias, chaenomeles, *Chimonanthus fragrans*, chionodoxas, *Choisya ternata*, *Clematis cirrhosa* var. *balearica*, *Cornus mas*, corylopsis, corylus, cowslips, crocus, daphnes, epimediums, *Eranthis hyemalis*, erysimums, euphorbias, *Garrya elliptica*, *Hamamelis mollis*, *Helleborus argutifolius*, *H. niger*, *H. foetidus*, *H. orientalis*, hepatica, *Iris histrioides*, *I. reticulata*, *I. unguicularis*, *Jasminum nudiflorum*, *Kerria japonica*, *Lonicera fragrantissima*, *Mahonia japonica*, *M. j.* Bealei Group, muscari, narcissus, oemleria, (nuttallia, osmaronia), osmanthus, *Pachyphragma macrophyllum*, pansies and violets, *Parrotia persica*, polyanthus, primulas, pulmonaria, *Puschkinia scilloides*, *Rubus spectabilis*, *Salix* spp. (catkins), sarcococca, scillas, snowdrops, *Symphytum grandiflorum*, tulip spp., viburnums *barclayana* germinate like mustard and cress and soon need pricking out. Another success, *Rehmannia elata*, I sowed from seed saved from a bought plant in March the following year. The rose-purple flowers have pale yellow throats with dark maroon spots. While in flower it makes quantities of underground offshoots, all ready to grow on for next January and February. Gertrude Jekyll recommends *Francoa ramosa* for growing in pots to stand on garden steps and other strategic places. They are easy to increase either from seed or by division during the winter.

The months after Christmas can be one of the busiest seasons in the vegetable garden. Each January we try – weather permitting – to get all the digging finished. The beds where peas and beans will be growing have plenty of manure incorporated. In February the early potatoes 'Home Guard' are 'put to chit' – laid out in boxes with the end with most eyes, called the rose end, upwards – so they are ready to plant out during the first week of March. Our planting system is to lay a sheet of black polythene on the ground, anchor it, then cut a series of crosses about 10 centimetres/4 inches across at 60-centimetre/2-foot intervals. We put a potato in each, half burying it in the soil, mound them up with peat and keep the whole area covered with clear perforated polythene (removed in early May) to protect the young shoots from early frost. Grown this way, each root does not have to be dug individually: we simply lift the black polythene and 'pick' the new potatoes, starting in early June.

By late February the lettuce and cauliflower seedlings should be big enough to pot on, and in mid-March, after hardening off, they can be put in the vegetable garden covered with cloches or fleece.

Early potatoes planted under black polythene have clear perforated poly as frost protection.

Then, too, we can sow the early carrots and perpetual spinach outside, covered with perforated polythene. The broad beans sown in November will be growing on and will need the support of shrub prunings.

In late February we plant the onion sets in trays in the greenhouse so they start growing roots; then by mid-March they are ready to go into their prepared beds. If you put them in without any roots the birds play havoc with them. A succession of peas, beans and lettuces will then be sown in order to keep the kitchen supplied throughout the summer.

As long as we did the planting last season, the winter harvest during these months will include sprouting broccoli, winter cabbage, Brussels sprouts and parsnips as well as red cabbage and leeks, and often some perpetual spinach. Some years we grow curly kale, a real stand-by in hard winters.

It is good to be able to slip away from home sometimes to attend the Royal Horticultural Society's shows in London. The early bulbs are always alluring and I enter in the garden book the ones I most admire; then, when autumn comes they can be ordered without further ado. An excitement in January and February comes with the *Iris reticulata*, to which I first paid close attention at one of the shows. Their markings are individual and wonderful. I try to buy a few of these each autumn, and find various places for them – in shallow pots, in tubs, or at the corners of the beds. Those in pots will be brought inside as they come into flower.

Keep your senses sharp through winter so you can relish all that nature has to offer you. The frost on your evergreens and cobwebs, the patterns on your lawn made by the slanting shadows, unexpected scent coming from winter-flowering shrubs – viburnums, chimonanthus, sarcococca – and that splash of gold from *Jasminum nudiflorum*. These are long-term pleasures, but with a little preparation in autumn you can have pools of white crocus and corners of *Iris reticulata* in your borders.

Groundsill, & all downy-plants) to run up to seede; for they will in a moment infect the whole ground: wherefore, whatever work you neglect, ply weedes at the first peeping of ye Spring. Malows, Thistles, Beanebind, Couch, must be grubb'd up and the ground forked & diligently pick'd.'

We fight a continual battle with our heritage of ground elder in this garden and paint it with Round-Up in April and May.

April and May

Spring for me starts when I see the leaf buds on the deciduous trees and shrubs swelling almost imperceptibly. This tells me that sap is rising, bringing the garden to life once again. The flowers of the first winter bulbs are already fading, but there are thousands more coming on, and everywhere there is fresh growth with precocious herbaceous plants sending up new leaves. I like spring to come slowly, with dignity, so I can enjoy every change, but each warm day brings an acceleration of growth. There must be sunshine so the flowers open to encourage the bees to collect the early pollen and nectar.

The Victorian greenhouse in April, the curved roof still covered with perforated polythene for insulation.

Caring for the lawns becomes a regular routine. They have an initial moss-killing treatment, then regular feeding combined with a spray to keep the broad-leaved weeds (plantain, daisy and buttercup) under control as mowing starts, using a cylinder mower. For weedkilling we have a splendid machine called a 'walkover', like a knapsack sprayer but on wheels: it makes sufficient impressions to indicate the lines of progress, and eliminates any time-consuming moving of string and markers.

After the selective weed-killing we hire a scarifier to

I allow myself plenty of time to 'stand and stare' and enjoy each changing mood, but there is always plenty to do. If you can stay up to date with your work programme now, the garden will look wonderful through early summer. We go round the borders regularly to dead head the tulips and narcissus and to keep on top of the weeds. Seedling weeds at a young stage will pull out easily – leave them to grow and they will take twice the time to eliminate. Follow John Evelyn's advice to his gardener:

'Above all, be carefull not to suffer weedes (especially Nettles, Dendelion,

churn up all the dead pieces and the thatch that has accumulated in the grass during last summer. This is not the best moment to appraise your lawn: in dismay you will wonder what you have done and whether it will ever recover. But several years ago, we bought a 'Billy Goat' – a sort of outdoor vacuum cleaner. It works like magic, picking up the awful debris that comes out of the lawn (it also saves hours of raking up fallen leaves in autumn).

Keeping the edges neat gives the garden that little extra tidy look. Once we used a special 'Spintrim' but its battery had to be recharged regularly, so we now use long-handled clippers: they get into awkward corners with greater agility than any machine.

Lawns are an essential part of our English gardens, and although I admire – probably envy – a perfect lawn, I am satisfied with our own, which has its quota of weeds, yet miraculously manages to look green throughout the summer despite hundreds of feet trampling on it. Some patches will need re-turfing, where too many visitors have trodden, or where we've allowed violas and other plants to spill over on to the lawn. We take turf from elsewhere or, if we have made a new flower bed, there will be turf to spare.

Through April and May the auriculas growing in a tub are at their best. More demanding than primulas, to me they are infinitely more rewarding. By the end of May, the tubs are demanding attention. The succession of bulbs is over and the various pelargoniums are waiting their turn to be brought out of their winter shelter. For years we have used an Ivy-leaved geranium, which we call "Best Mauve", together with half-hardy helichrysum and a few scented-leaved geraniums. We also have Ivy-leaved *Pelargonium* 'Hederinum', which we brought back as cuttings from a plant flowering

To me, auriculas are the most beautiful spring flowers, with subtle colours and defined markings.

profusely on our balcony at a hotel in Normandy. The blooms start a bright pink, then fade in harmony so there are always two colours glowing. We plant tightly so that all summer the effect will be one of overflowing. With these tubs close to my doorway I have a feeling of summer exuberance immediately I walk out into the garden. Tubs that live on the verandah have a yellow theme to complement the honey colour of the Cotswold stone. The yellow daisy-flowered *Bidens ferulifolia* clambers through *Helichrysum petiolare*, surrounding golden variegated box; combinations that are long-lasting and satisfying.

Other tubs around the garden are filled with salvias and diascias. James Compton brought back many wonderful salvias from expeditions to Mexico – you can see them at Newby Hall in Yorkshire (his parents' home) – and Dan Hinkley gave me several from his Heronswood Nurseries near Seattle. The vivid blue *Salvia patens* we grow from seed each year and plant liberally on corners of the beds and in important places where their strong colour will be a feature all through the summer. The unusual salvias must be well guarded. The stock plants are grown in tubs where rampant annuals or perennials in the borders will not smother them. I know I will never be a specialist in any species or have the patience to create a superlative rock garden, so the treasures friends give me must have secure homes. I would hate to lose them.

The pleasure garden and the potager take turns in needing the most attention. The daffodils, and later the tulips, will be bowing out in the borders, and where these are finally over we can add our summer mainstay of penstemons, erysimums, nicotianas, salvias and lobelias. With all the preparation for summer, we must also keep longer-term plans in mind. There is continuous seed sowing, sometimes in plugs and sometimes, as the soil warms up, in prepared seed beds. If we can get sweet rocket, aquilegias, delphiniums, lupins and lots of others growing on in early summer, they will make good flowering plants for next year. In May we are busy in the potager planting out as many seedlings as possible. There are always vegetables to pick, allowing me to spend time in the potager, contemplating future plans.

The air is full of anticipation, for early summer will soon burst upon us, bringing more work and more flowers.

June and July

A special occasion is when the garden opens for the National Gardens Scheme the first Saturday in June, with the laburnum tunnel in full bloom.

The change in the character of the garden from May to early June is dramatic and involves us working through every bed. The forget-me-nots, now past their best, are pulled out and put into the chicken run to make future compost; the cowslips and primulas are dug, divided and lined out into a shady corner in the potager, to be ready to use again next autumn. Most have their seed heads cut off, but we keep enough that have good colours to ripen. We leave in the tulips under the laburnums, between hostas and under deciduous shrubs; other tulips are dug, put into boxes and covered with soil so they can dry off naturally. The plants we have hardened off – the salvias, penstemons, lobelias, diascias and any annuals large enough – are planted into the empty spaces. Pansies and violas make a great contribution at this moment, before the perennials come into flower. The spring look has gone, making way for early summer.

Les in April placing pots of Salvia patens *with* Parahebe lyallii *for colour in July.*

We heed John Evelyn's advice – '*Never expose yr Oranges, Limons, and like tender plants whatever season flatter 'til the Mulberry puts forth its leafe*' – and watch our mulberry. We only have one lemon tree, but Evelyn's wisdom can be applied to other tender plants. The *Echeveria* 'Imbricata' are dropped into some corners of the borders to make a pretty tapestry with bronze-leaved ajuga and under evergreen hebes. The white daisy, *Argyranthemum frutescens*, saved from last year and overwintered indoors, are arranged in a bold mass mixed with dark red penstemons. The *Francoa ramosa* are taken out

of the greenhouse, divided where necessary and repotted. Those for sale will be put in plastic pots, ours to keep into old 25-centimetre/10-inch terracotta ones to stand on steps and round the garden all summer. They will flower in August and September. Other clay containers which were used for spring bulbs are now filled with felicia and fuchsias, already in flower. The Victorian greenhouse, full to capacity all winter with pelargoniums, felicias, fuchsias and succulents, must be kept tidy and free of whitefly. This is easier said than done – we spray regularly, alternating each time with a different deterrent, and also keep sticky yellow strips hanging. This does not work as well as it should, so I am considering using the recommended predators.

Certain jobs come up almost daily, others weekly. The paths round the garden are swept on Mondays. If it has been windy and a lot of debris is about, the Billy Goat comes out. Mowing and edging are inevitable. I once paced out the edges and discovered we have more than 900 yards – over half a mile (around 830 metres) – so they don't all get done every week!

By July most of the gaps in the borders will have been filled, but I go round with a gardener most days. I take a diary and make notes about work to be done, and we have clippers and a bucket to do any minor dead-heading as we go. Flowers such as campanulas and daisies will continue to open more buds if they are kept dead-headed. Others, like *Phlomis russeliana*, form lovely seed heads, so we allow these to stay. Some we must take off, for if left they will seed unmercifully. These include the *Allium aflatunense* under the laburnums and the angelica round the fountain. Instinct tells me when the lady's mantle, *Alchemilla mollis*, and the sweet cicely,

Myrrhis odorata, must be cut severely to the ground, just before their seeds ripen and proliferate through the garden. Then they are watered and mulched to encourage new growth; both will produce a carpet of fresh young leaves in a few days.

Another category flowers only once and then displays fading leaves. The oriental poppies and *Geranium pratense* are among these. They flower at the same time and then by mid-July are gone, so their leaves are cut to the ground and penstemons from the selling yard are carefully dropped in between them to flower in late summer surrounded by the new poppy and geranium leaves. We collect the seeds of many other plants. Some are stored to be sown next year and others are sown straight away in seed beds, although not all will germinate until the following spring.

A note will go in the diary to summer prune the June-flowering philadelphus, weigela and the American beauty bush, *Kolkwitzia amabilis*, to be done any time from now on. Cutting out many of the branches that have produced flowers allows energy to go into the new growth on which next year's flowers will bloom. We also make notes about what cutting material is ready to keep the mist propagator filled. Sometimes I wish I was computer-minded so we could flash on to a screen exactly how many cuttings are rooting and already for sale, but I know I must rely on my memory.

The selling yard has to be stocked up with plants from the cow yard, the tunnel and elsewhere, usually on Mondays and Fridays. On busy Saturdays in June and July we need three people on duty to attend to visitors wanting help. As plants are sold, gaps are filled with a selection of whatever is in flower or looking good in the garden at the time, and what we know people will want to buy.

June and July are busy months in the vegetable garden, sowing,

Red Brussels sprouts grown from seeds are lined out by Andy in the potager in June.

planting out and harvesting. Every year is slightly different, but the general pattern of routine remains the same. We try to keep a succession of lettuce sown, and sow runner beans, more French beans, main-crop beetroot, carrots, marrows and courgettes, spinach and spinach beet. The white and purple sprouting broccoli and Brussels sprouts, leeks, sweet corn and cauliflower, winter and red cabbage seedlings we sowed in May either outside or in plugs will be ready to plant out. We aim to keep each area filled, keeping to the crop rotation of peas and beans followed by brassicas, followed by roots. Seedling weeds, mostly annuals, must be pulled up; at last, after hand weeding for years, we have got rid of most of the perennials like dandelions and thistles.

I like a mixture of flowers among the vegetables. The standard roses 'Little White Pet' have to be carefully dead-headed; some of the well established hollyhocks, self-seeded from an original sowing in the seed bed, grow well over head height. The yellow Welsh poppies have seeded into odd corners and grow through the box edging. This is clipped in early July, after the box in the flower garden is finished, and takes many hours to do. There are the hawthorns to prune back as well, any time after they have finished flowering. The hedge has its castellated look and the standards are in large balls.

August and September

The exuberance of our borders in June and July quietens by early August. Plants settle into slower growth, some perennials begin to look tired, and the later-flowering daisies come into their own. The borders are still overflowing, but do not imagine that the garden can be left to its own devices.

This is the time to look critically at borders, early in the morning or in the evening, when the light is clear but not too bright, making notes of colour associations that please you. A good combination for the front rank is pink diascias and blue felicias, which flower continuously if you dead head them and blend well with mauve and blue violas. My notes suggest an accompaniment of grey *Artemisia stelleriana* or *A. alba* 'Canescens'. Also take time to appraise the form and habit of taller plants and their contribution to a border. At Barnsley we keep staking to a minimum, but some plants – acanthus, tall lobelias, monkshoods and the annual lavateras 'Mont Blanc' and 'Silver Cup' – definitely benefit from support by individual bamboos. The growth of many perennials varies from year to year according to the rainfall. *Anthemis tinctoria* 'E.C. Buxton' can grow to 1.2 metres/4 feet and as this yellow daisy flowers non-stop until severe frosts, it is well worth staking plants individually.

The day-to-day diaries reiterate the routine jobs – pruning, dead-heading, tidying round, taking cuttings. The long arms sent out by the wisteria growing on the house and those through the laburnum walk must be cut back to two buds, otherwise flowers will not develop next year. I always think that hollies root best when cuttings are taken in August or September, so where they are grown as 'topiary' they can be shaped now, and the clippings used as hardwood cuttings. I am surprised so few people appreciate how easy it is to increase their stock of shrubs. We have made a bed of well-drained sandy soil on the north-west side of a walk and use this every year for hardwood cuttings of ribes, spiraea, weigela, golden and silver privet, rue, rosemary, hebes, golden- and red-stemmed cornus and all the willows. In winter the bed is covered with perforated polythene to keep off the worst of the

Andy at work in early July, clipping the box edging in the potager.

weather. We also take cuttings of semi-ripe wood of lavender; through experience we have found that almost a hundred per cent of them will root if taken now. Climbing roses are put in when the thorns break off cleanly without tearing the skin of the stem.

The laburnums must be dead headed if they were not done earlier – the seeds are extremely poisonous. We go round the limes to take off any new growth spoiling their symmetry and keep them well tutored. The *Lonicera nitida* hedge by the entrance to the car park has its second clipping, and the golden *L.n.* 'Baggesen's Gold' grown as pouffes around the bases of the lime trunks is given a haircut. At the same time the matching ivies on these limes are kept strictly to 45 centimetres/18 inches. I do not want them any higher. We also shape the yew hedges with electric clippers in August. The beech hedge is done later.

In the flower borders a regular August/September job is cutting back the violas, especially the *Viola cornuta* and other special varieties like *V.* 'Atalanta' and *V.* 'Belmont Blue'. They are given a feed of phostrogen or a mulch and very soon will make appreciable new growth which can be used for cuttings. The rock roses on the central path between the Irish yews are also cut back – clipping them to just above the new growth – and again these young shoots make ideal cutting material.

If the weather is fine, then all the tubs and containers must have a good watering at least once a week, and we feed them a final boost of fertilizer for the autumn to supplement the Vitex Q4 added to their compost when they were planted at the end of May and which lasts about three months. We are also experimenting with using a liquid feed made from comfrey leaves that is rich in potash for our pot plants and tubs.

The outer scales of the honesty seed heads will come off readily now, leaving the shining 'silver pennies', which look wonderful in a group with the sun shining through them. Other seeds are also gathered as they ripen. Perhaps we make work for ourselves by collecting our own seeds to sow at the appropriate time, grow on and then pot up to sell – all using valuable gardening time.

There are wet-day jobs other than sorting seed, potting and taking cuttings. The bulbs that were put to dry off in late spring must be cleaned and got ready to plant once again. It is vital that they are labelled accurately.

The gardeners are busy in the vegetable garden, with much help from my grandson Anthony. The tops of the ripe onions are bent over, all in one direction to look efficient. During a warm spell they are pulled out of the ground and allowed finally to dry off thoroughly before being stored. More winter brassicas are planted in every available space, and we plant out as many lettuces as we can.

A 2.4-metre/8-foot sunflower 'Mammoth' towers over the apple tunnel in the potager.

The plums and gooseberries must be kept picked, and so must the autumn raspberries. Unless they are netted, the currants are taken by the birds. I regret not having enough space for a regular fruit cage, hidden away where it will not spoil the decorative effect of the potager. Strawberry beds receive their quota of attention. If we want new plants, we allow the necessary number of runners to root before severing them and potting them on or planting them out in a new bed. The old bed is thoroughly cleaned and mulched with cocoa-shell.

We are always longing to be able to summer prune the apples. We were told by Bonham Bazeley of Highfield Nurseries that we must wait to cut back the current year's growth until the leaf on the tip of this has developed, otherwise our work will be wasted and the goodness which should go into flowers and fruit buds will go into new leaves. So we keep to the letter of Bonham's Law and usually find that we can spur back these growths to two buds by mid-August. This makes the trees much more effective, shows their training and also allows extra light in to encourage the fruit to ripen. Basically fruit tree pruning is all logical – once you have mastered the facts – but each tree and bush presents a different problem, we find. You must be bold with the clippers and at the same time make sure you recognize fruit buds.

In September, just as in April, general maintenance must be kept at a high level of workmanship, but now every day there will be touches of autumn, leaves yellowing and some falling. Beneath, late-blooming flowers shine and complement the autumn colours of the foliage.

October, November and December

How lucky we are to garden in England, where we have four very different seasons. Yet each year the exact pattern is slightly different. Some years light frosts bring outstanding autumn colour, with leaves hanging on in their finery until mid-November. We look at the birch by the tennis court and the limes up the drive and wonder if the leaves will ever fall, while the Turkey oak and wisteria leaves may cling on into December. Some autumns a helpful wind blows the dry fallen leaves and piles them up effortlessly into a corner or against a wall so they are easy to clear up. Other years, wet, still days mean an almost daily raking and Billy Goating to prevent a heavy carpet of damp plane and chestnut leaves from covering the emerging bulbs and winter aconites.

Fallen leaves have no nutrient value, but when they are gathered and rotted down for a year they become precious humus. The secret is to make sure that every fresh gathering added to the wire enclosure is thoroughly damp – dry leaves will not rot. As autumn merges into winter and this year's leaves are gathered, last year's rotted leaves are added generously to the borders in the form of lush brown leaf mould. Thanks to our visit to the Henry Doubleday Research Association, we now also keep back enough bags of leaf mould to mix with chopped comfrey leaves, making perfect seed-sowing compost. The leaf mould provides good drainage and the comfrey's supply of vital potash gives a great boost to our seedlings.

We all enjoy autumn work on the borders. The feeling of summer urgency is over and we can put our minds to planting bulbs, dividing perennials, making changes. We like to work through all the borders before Christmas – it is risky to leave the tidying up and planting any later, as frost and snow in January and February often make it impossible to get on to the ground. New plants then have time to become established, and we have a great feeling of satisfaction when everything is tidy, all the bulbs are safely planted, and the spaces between them filled with sturdy young plants of forget-me-nots, love-in-a-mist and cowslips. We order the bulbs early, usually in August, and store them safely in the barn. One rainy day, a gardener and I have a session studying previous bulb lists and planting places. We take an hour or so to write the desti-

nation on each bag of bulbs, which saves time and mistakes in the garden. As each bag becomes empty, we imagine next spring's colourful display.

My philosophy is to give each border a thorough overhaul every three years (sooner if need be) so the more delicate specimens are not taken over by the spreaders. It is easy to lose a small, valuable plant through unintentional neglect. Even the sturdier perennials – like clumps of monarda and *Phlomis russeliana* – perform better once dug and divided. The day lilies are split at least every three years to keep them flowering prolifically. Periodically our acanthus gets quite out of hand, so much of it is carefully dug up and potted on for the nursery; even a small piece of root will shoot again. *Lamium maculatum* are wonderful front-of-the-border plants but they must be restrained.

After cutting down worn herbaceous stems and tidying shrubs comes one of the best moments – when the brown leaf mould is spread liberally over the beds as a mulch, giving a final touch of perfection, so when the bulbs come through they look wonderful against their rich, well-cared-for carpet of humus. This is also the time to keep an eye open for mice, which nip the fresh young crocus shoots while they are still below ground. We put out mouse-traps covered by inverted wooden boxes, making sure that robins cannot creep under them and get caught. The traps are looked at daily. The tally one year between bulb planting and Christmas was thirty-six – if each mouse had eaten its quota, think how many crocus we would have lost.

Seed to be sown when fresh

Aconitum 'Ivorine', *Althaea officinalis*, astrantia, campanulas, cowslips, cyclamen, delphiniums, *Dianthus* 'Loveliness', digitalis, eremurus, *Eryngium giganteum*, helianthemums, *Helleborus argutifolius*, *H. orientalis*, *Hesperis matronalis*, hollyhocks, honesty, hostas, *Lychnis coronaria* Alba Group, *Malva alcea* var. *fastigiata*, *Morina longifolia*, *M. afghanica*, *Oenothera biennis*, polemonium, Barnhaven polyanthus, *P. denticulata*, gold laced polyanthus, *Rudbeckia triloba*, *Salvia argentea*, *S. glutinosa*, *S. sclarea* var. *turkestanica*, *Sidalcea malviflora*, *Silybum marianum*, *Thalictrum aquilegiifolium*, *Verbascum bombyciferum*, *V. phoeniceum*, *Viola* 'Bowles' Black'

Seed gathered for sowing the following spring

Abutilon × suntense, *Aconitum carmichaelii* 'Arendsii', *Dictamnus albus* var. *purpureus*, *D. fraxinella*, *Dierama pulcherrimum*, *Eccremocarpus scaber*, *Francoa ramosa*, *Galega officinalis*, *Ipomoea* 'Heavenly Blue', *Lavatera* 'Mont Blanc', *Lavatera arborea* 'Variegata', *Lophospermum erubescens*, *Nicotiana langsdorffii*, *N. sylvestris*, *Pulsatilla vulgaris*, *Rhodochiton atrosanguineus*, *Rudbeckia* 'Marmalade', *Salvia patens*, sweet peas, *Tropaeolum peregrinum*, *Viola cornuta*

Important autumn work is to make sure we have taken cuttings of all the half-hardy plants we acquired and enjoyed in the summer. If we could only predict how severe the winter would be, our horticultural life would be easier. But we must ensure that our favourite salvias, verbenas, felicias, helichrysums and bidens are perpetuated. I think I owe this not only to myself but also to the clients who come here in springtime to stock their gardens. If I lose plants, other nurseries may do also.

Between 'doing the beds', we choose a warm calm day when the plants can stand outside without harm to prepare the greenhouses for winter. Luckily the three greenhouses are small enough to make it possible to do one in a day. The walls are hosed down and Jeyes Fluid is applied to the floor and into every corner, in the hope of getting rid of any lurking whitefly. The glass is cleaned to allow a maximum of our feeble winter light to come through. Cracks in the glass of the Victorian house let in cold air, so for economy of heating we line it with bubble plastic, which means we cannot open the roof ventilators. Every plant is taken care of. Some are cut back to make them into a better, more compact shape, and when necessary they are repotted. The cuttings are trimmed, carefully labelled and put into rooting mixture. We put a table down the centre of the main greenhouse and everything is tightly packed in. Some years we have a problem with high humidity and daily vigilance is necessary to prevent mildew; we take off every yellowing leaf and dead flower, and use fans to keep the air circulating.

A task for October is to trim the beech hedge along the back of the wilderness. This is quite tough on the electric clippers and will take two or three days to do well. Then the moment comes when the summer tubs and containers have had their day and the bulbs we have allocated for them are ready and waiting to be planted. First the pelargoniums, bidens, helichrysum and any other plants are carefully taken out; some will be potted up and have cuttings taken. Then the soil is dug out almost to the bottom and replaced with a barrowload of freshly mixed compost – a mixture of three parts of sieved compost from the hen run to one each of peat and perlite, with Vitax Potting Base added. A good layer of crocks at the bottom ensures drainage.

At the edge of the bed a board protects the lawn while tulip bulbs are laid out ready for planting.

Often a tub has a holly or box as a centrepiece. First the chosen tulips, probably twenty or so, are put in, then covered with compost, and narcissus are added on top. We then fill the tubs to within a short distance of the top and a mixed layer of 'Paper White' narcissus and *chrysanthus crocus* is planted together. In the past we topped up with vincas or pansies for interest while waiting for the crocus to bloom in early February, but the 'Paper Whites' have been a successful alternative: they flower within six weeks of planting and stay looking and smelling lovely until the first hard frost. We gather moss from our walls and other stones and add it like a well-tucked-in shawl all across the top, for the bulbs to push their way through.

When does autumn end and winter start, and how many months are there in these seasons? It does not matter: it is good to be able to walk round the garden and know that we are working, daily, to our goal of having the borders finished by Christmas. This means that in the New Year we can get on with all the other jobs I have in mind that will contribute to the well-being of the garden.

Index

Page numbers in italics refer to illustrations and their captions

Author's Acknowledgments

The story of the garden at Barnsley House has been in my mind for several years. Many people have helped directly or indirectly with its creation. First over the years I must mention my father- and mother-in-law, Cecil and Linda Verey, who gave us Barnsley House in 1951. Ever in my thoughts is my late husband David, who shared with me the pleasures and planning of the garden.

More recently, Andrew Lawson, Tony Lord and Jerry Harpur have through their skilful photography opened my eyes to the progressive changes in the garden.

I thank the staff at Frances Lincoln for their expertise and their kindness; Tony Lord for photographing the garden in its different moods for this book; all my gardeners past and present; my gardening friends who have contributed ideas; Katherine Lambert for interpreting my words; and above all my family, who love and enjoy the garden.

Publishers' Acknowledgments

Frances Lincoln Publishers thank Penny David for help with the text and Jean Bayfield, Margherita Gianni and Gareth Richards for their assistance with text, artwork and index. For the black-and-white illustrations the Publishers are grateful to the author and Hilary Wills. The photographs on pages 6 to 11 were taken by members of the Verey family, with a home box brownie.

Editors *Alison Freegard, Sarah Mitchell*
Art Editor *Patricia Going*
Horticultural consultants *Antonia Johnson, Tony Lord*
Picture Editor *Anne Fraser*
Production *Annemarieke Kroon*
Editorial Director *Erica Hunningher*
Art Director *Caroline Hillier*
Production Director *Nicky Bowden*